Balancing Public and Private Health Care Systems

The Sub-Saharan African Experience

Randolph Quaye

D1065934

UNIVERSITY PRESS OF AMERICA,® INC.
Lanham • Boulder • New York • Toronto • Plymouth, UK

Copyright © 2010 by
University Press of America,® Inc.
4501 Forbes Boulevard
Suite 200
Lanham, Maryland 20706
UPA Acquisitions Department (301) 459-3366

Estover Road
Plymouth PL6 7PY
United Kingdom

All rights reserved
Printed in the United States of America
British Library Cataloging in Publication Information Available

Library of Congress Control Number: 2009935805
ISBN: 978-0-7618-4930-8 (paperback : alk. paper)
eISBN: 978-0-7618-4931-5

∞ ™ The paper used in this publication meets the minimum
requirements of American National Standard for Information
Sciences—Permanence of Paper for Printed Library Materials,
ANSI/NISO Z39.48-1992.

Contents

Preface

Since the publication of my first book, *Underdevelopment and Health Care in Africa* (1996), much has changed in the way SubSaharan Africans finance health care. In the best of times, funding for the health sectors has come from general taxation, donor support, and private out-of-pocket payments. Yet the health services are woefully underfunded, and access to health care has been a major problem for Africans. This situation has been further compounded by social and economic marginalization fuelled by both internal economic underdevelopment and external forces of economic dependency and crippling state debt. At the same time, of the 43.3 million people in the world who were living with AIDS in 2001, 24.5 million were in SubSaharan Africa. Of the 13.2 million children orphaned by that time by AIDS, 95 percent were in Africa (Gysels, Pool and Nnalusiba, 2002). Household spending on health care has amounted to almost half of all Sub Saharan Africa health care expenditure and yet, regrettably, the majority of the African population does not have adequate access to health care (Schieber and Maeda, 1997). So what is wrong then?

In response to World Bank recommendation that the principle of cost recovery or out-of-pocket contributions by individuals or users of health care services be included in any healthcare financing strategies, African countries embraced the principle of private-public partnership in health care. It was argued then, and still now that a way out of their health conundrum is for governments to play a smaller role in providing health services by requiring citizens to pay or pay more for public services.

While specific country case studies on health have been presented in the literature, relatively little comparative work has been done on private healthcare financing, and especially in West and East Africa. The present book, *Balancing Public and Private Health Care Systems: The Sub-Saharan*

African Experience, explores the different financing arrangements tried in Ghana, Tanzania, and Uganda. It introduces new scholarship on post-colonial health care strategies in Africa, especially during a decade of market-oriented healthcare reforms. Specifically, it attempts to explain why in nearly all African countries, "Demands from international donors for increased efficiency and competition are leading governments to play a smaller role in providing health care" (Panos Report, 1994: 1). The 1990s have accurately been described as the decade of market reforms in health care in the West and East Africa. As for Africa, in the first decade of the 21st century, a confluence of forces has changed the nature of healthcare financing in unprecedented ways. While one form of cost sharing (user fees), has been used extensively in Africa, the nature of its use and its type of healthcare financing have differed across the continent. Some African countries have depended on community health care financing schemes such as those in Tanzania and Kenya, but relatively little is known about the history of this or other social health care insurance as a financing strategy in Africa. Both Tanzania and Ghana have relatively short history of using social government health insurance as a financing option. As for Uganda, it does not currently have any social health insurance in place, although its feasibility is being explored.

Drawing upon current research and case studies, as well as recent work by the author himself on African healthcare systems, this book sets out to analyze the implications of the various strategies for the future of healthcare financing in Africa. The book appears at a timely moment, given widespread current discussion about equity in health care and the role of the state in healthcare planning.

My work was supported by the Ohio Wesleyan University TEW Presidential Discretionary Fund. Chapter One has appeared in slightly different form in the *Journal of Social Theory and Health*. Chapter Three appeared in a modified version in the *International Journal of Health Care Quality Assurance*. I thank both editors for permission to rework these two articles.

My thanks are also due to many others: Professor Joseph Wang'ombe of the Department of Community Medicine at the University of Nairobi for his interest in my work and for providing relevant resources. Dr. Edward Kumira, Dean of the Faculty, Makerere University for taking time to discuss African healthcare with me; Dr Robert Basaza, Health Economist and Isabela Ndibalekera, both at the Ugandan Ministry of Health, for their resourcefulness and their willingness to share relevant documents with me.

A special thank you is owed my brother, Daniel Jeremy Quaye Jnr, and to Asare Awuku, Dinah Quarm, Agnes Bonney, and the rest of the Bonney and Quaye families. To Kwesi Kofi, Kojo Kobina, Asi and Mama Felicia Awuku, I thank you for your forbearance during the writing of this book. This book was completed during a painful period in my life. On January 29, 2009, my mother, Dora Bonney, passed away, followed on April 5, 2009, by my father, Daniel Jeremy Quaye Snr. I regret that they did not live to see the completion of this project but I learned the courage and determination so evident in their lives to carry on this important research. For that, I dedicate this book to my beloved parents.

Introduction

The goal of providing universal access to health care, based upon the Universal Declaration of Human Rights, is a laudable one. In most Western societies, this goal has been achieved through general taxation, private insurance, and by government's sponsoring healthcare financing programs like individual and community sickness savings and voluntary and private and state compulsory insurance plans. But in nearly all African countries, politicians and citizens alike have been disappointed with their healthcare delivery systems. Most Africans do not have adequate access to health care, and private healthcare services are beyond the reach of a great many. The poor quality of medical care in public facilities leave much to be desired and yet year after year government attempts to rectify this situation have not materialized.

Furthermore in the past two decades, demands from international donors for increased efficiency and competition have forced governments to play a smaller role in providing health care. As eloquently noted by Agyepong (1999:3), "Policies that encourage the development of the private health sector can widen access to health care to the population, but system–wide inefficiencies can occur if the public and private health sectors are not integrated."

This book explores the different healthcare financing initiatives introduced in three Sub Saharan African countries in the early 1990s and examines how effective these reforms have been in addressing the broader goals of access, equity, efficiency and effectiveness in health care along with the social and health implications of such reforms for the lives of citizens of these countries. Although there is a great deal of international support for cost sharing in health care, it must be noted that the very essence of such an approach endangers the principles that formed the basis of these reforms in the first place. The book concludes by calling on African governments to identity 'best practices" in healthcare financing and to develop programs to overcome the ill effects of such policies on the lives of vulnerable groups in their societies.

Chapter One presents the evolution of healthcare policy in Sub Saharan Africa, with a particular focus on private healthcare financing. The various health care financing strategies are debated with an eye towards exploring how they intersect with the particular circumstances of each country studied.

Chapter Two explores how these financing strategies affect hospital attendance and the wider issue of equity in health care. It examines the literature on cost recovery in general and the special case of user fees in health care. It makes the point that cost sharing in whatever form is highly burdensome for people with low incomes and in fact has disastrous consequences for the delivery and utilization of health services by most of the population. Chapter Three considers the feasibility of introducing government health insurance in Kenya and Uganda and the challenges it faces. Chapter Four presents evidence from Ghana on the effects of its introduction of health insurance in 2003.

Chapter Five in Tanzanian investigates the history of healthcare financing and assesses the role of private and public health insurance in health care delivery there. Chapter Six discusses the role and success of community health care funding in meeting health needs, especially of rural and farming communities in Tanzania. Chapter Seven considers healthcare financing strategies from other countries and summarizes findings on state health insurance and the role of community health funding in health care delivery systems in SubSaharan Africa.

Chapter One

Crisis and Change in African Health Care Financing Systems

PAYING FOR HEALTH CARE SERVICES IN SUB SAHARAN AFRICA: HISTORICAL OVERVIEW

The early 1990s can aptly be described as the decade of market-oriented reforms in health care. Most European countries, in an attempt to reduce mounting healthcare costs, initiated several market reforms with the goal of expanding healthcare coverage at lower cost (Quaye, 2004). Thus, in African countries in the past decade, there has been increasing focus on, and concern about, the quality of medical care, financial constraints and the problem of access and equity in health care. Cost sharing through user fees have been used extensively in Africa, with mixed results. This change in financing healthcare was the direct result of decades of African economic decline, debt crises and political instability that led to the implementation of so called structural adjustment programs.

Historically, Africans and their governments have been disappointed with the performance of their health service delivery. The prevailing healthcare care system, modelled after the Western medical system with its emphasis on hospital and curative care, has failed to deal effectively with the major causes of death. Malnutrition, a chronic state of malnourishment caused by deficient intake of calories explains much of the high mortality and morbidity statistics in Africa (Quaye, 1991). In the last decade, approximately seventy percent of the healthcare budgets in Sub Saharan African countries has gone to curative medicine, while a mere 10 percent has been allocated for preventive care. Resources have been allocated for the urban few at the expense of the poor mostly rural majority. This maldistribution of health resources has major implications for the average health status of Africans. The available demographic information on malnutrition, life expectancy and mortality are

1

disturbing consequences of failed healthcare system. The poor populations health status in East and West Africa is of course further complicated by the economic crises and the fiscal deficits faced by African governments.

The dependence of so many Sub Saharan African governments on a single cash crop or other primary products for export to fund major development projects has had serious consequences. Given the fact that agricultural exports alone account for 65 percent of Sub Saharan total export earnings, a decline in the terms of trade ,especially in agricultural products, have serious repercussions for the economies of these countries as occurred in the early 1980s. As a result of recession in the Western world, African economies witnessed substantial declines. Both internal political conditions (such as fragility of democratic institutions, civil wars and external economic constraints imposed by adverse terms of trade) led to a substantial decrease in earnings.

The failure of the African states to resolve and respond effectively to both foreign and local class interests eroded the state's hold on the economy. Many Sub Saharan African countries balked at the International Monetary Fund's (IMF) initial stabilization programs. But by the end of the 1980s, the debt crisis had precipitated drastic changes in the African continent under pressure from public and private foreign creditors (Quaye, 1991). These programs were designed to reduce the basic imbalances between state revenues and expenses through such measures as wage freezes, devaluation of currencies, removal of subsidies, and reduction in state expenditures on social services (Cornia et al., 1990). Many SubSaharan African governments as part of this policy, African governments pursued a retrenchment policy in which government workers were laid off.

A major consequence of IMF stabilization was the introduction for the first time in African countries cost sharing or user fees in healthcare services. The Ministry of Health in Kenya in 1989 established cost sharing for government hospitals and health centers (Huber, 1993). Approximately 14 out of 15 African countries surveyed by Gilson and Russell (1995) have introduced user fees. A review of the literature to be discussed in Chapter Three identified two models. According to Gilson and Russell (1995), the standard model has among its objectives the need to make health services more efficient and equitable. In that regard, the goal was to introduce sector changes and other incentive methods to ensure efficient delivery of health services by healthcare providers. This has the intended goal of protecting the most vulnerable in society. For example, the Kenyan government in its goal to achieve equity issued a policy directive to exempt the poor (Wang'ombe et al, 2002). The second approach is the Bamako Initiative (BI).

The Bamako Initiative approach is widely used now in Tanzania through its community financing program with community involvement and decentralization of health services. As Jarrett and Ofosu-Amaah (1992: 65) noted, the Bamako Initiative "is a strategy designed towards the long- term sustainability of primary health care into the next century." Its aim is for governments to "curtail their expenditure on hospitals and highly trained personnel and devote more resources to the staffing of low-level health "(Criel, 1998: 4). As clearly documented (Mwabu et al., 1998, 2002, Criel, 1998, Gilson and Russell, 1997), user fees are highly regressive. As Criel (1998:40) noted,' User fees create particular programs for farmers for whom income is highly seasonal." In Ghana, Kenya, Tanzania and Uganda, user fees have been associated with a decline in attendance at hospitals and clinics (Mwabu and Wang'ombe, 1998; Mwabu et al., 1996; Collins et al., 1996). Particularly, Mwabu reported in the Kenyan experience that the fees led to reduced attendance at government health facilities by 40-50 percent.

Another objective of user fees has been to reduce unnecessary use of health services. Asking users to pay a portion of their health service, no matter how nominal the fee, is intended to discourage excessive use of such services. This has the perverse impact of discouraging the poor from seeking basic health care. After all, less than five percent of recurrent expenditures is recovered from user fees (Quaye, 2004). In the light of this, use of income from user fees to support health care financing schemes has been quite disappointing.

What follows will briefly but critically examines the implementation of these market reforms in different health care financing schemes and assesses them in light of available data with regard to the central issues of health care equity, efficiency and accessibility in Kenya, Uganda and Tanzania Later chapters will explore the various alternative reforms in more detail in specific countries.

KENYA'S EXPERIENCE WITH HEALTH CARE FINANCING

Health insurance has been used extensively in Western societies and it constitutes the major share of healthcare financing. This is not the case in Africa. Kenya provides a good example of the role of health insurance in health care. The available literature suggests that health insurance schemes pose several problems for governments. One major drawback is its limited coverage. For example, the only –well established insurance is the National Hospital Insurance Fund (NHIF). This insurance covers only those in the public sector. According to Wang'ombe, the current insurance and other insurance schemes covers only 20 percent of the population. The study also concluded that only 3 percent of Kenyan households actually used insurance to pay for medical services. The study further confirmed that because of the limited coverage and the long delays in reimbursement from the National Hospital Insurance Fund (NHIF), several patients were less likely to use insurance to pay for medical care in public hospitals. They also reported that patients were generally dissatisfied with the services that they received from government hospitals (Wang'ombe et al., 2002).

The Kenyan experience does suggest that insurance programs by themselves do not adequately address the barrier to access. In some cases, as borne out by the Kenyan study, it might actually discourage the timely utilization of health services with severe implications for health. Another drawback in terms of the use of insurance is that it is by its very nature regressive. In other African countries, governments prefer a flat rate contribution than that based on need and income earnings. This suggests that a large number of Africans who utilize the health services do so with their own money. As a matter of fact, personal health spending accounts for almost half of all health care expenditure in Africa. This does not bode well for increased insurance use in health care. Geographical locations also limit the use of insurance. Most of the insurance plans are for employees in the formal sector. These employees mostly live in urban centers. However, large segments of the population working from the informal economic sector live in rural communities, making health insurance availability a tall order.

THE UGANDAN EXPERIENCE

In a paper titled, "A Feasibility Analysis of Social Insurance in Uganda" a team from the Harvard University School of Public Health and the Ugandan Institute of Public Health concluded that while social insurance can improve health performance in Uganda, the "conditions prevailing in Uganda as in many low-income countries may make the successful development of social health insurance [SHI] difficult and risky" (Government of Uganda, 2001: 7). The next logical question is why? The study observed that the problem for Uganda is not the will, but the revenue to support such a program. They estimated that in 1999/2000, the total expenditure was equal to 20.7 percent of GDP, while the total revenue was only 11.9 percent. While external budget supports 30 percent of total government expenditure, such reliance on external sources creates problems for effective planning and raises questions of "Sustainability and affordability" (The Republic of Uganda, 2000). A quick review of funding sources indicates that about 43 percent of the total sources of revenue come from donors (internal and external), households contribute 34 percent, employers contribute 3 percent and 30 percent came from the government (Ministry of Health, 2000). This shows that increasingly, the

Ugandan government is playing a smaller role in this area and yet at the same time, has a wider mandate for promoting health services. Perhaps, this explains why in March 2001, the government abolished user fees in health care. What is also clear is that the poor contribute 27.4 percent to healthcare expenditure. The major source of revenue for the government is from income tax revenues. This is obtained from 27 percent of individuals in the private and parastatal sector, and from 16.5 percent of civil servants (Government of Uganda, 2001: 18).

About 91 percent of total donor contributions go mainly to finance primary health care, while over 58 percent of total government funding is allocated to the national referral hospitals serving 15 percent of the population (Government of Uganda, 2001). Uganda, like other African countries, faces similar problems with access. The utilization of services is reported to be low, especially among rural populations. They attribute these delays to transportation costs and the inability to pay for services. The quandary for most patients is that even though user fees have been abolished, the limited availability of drugs and the long delays and poor quality of service make virtually all users in practice pay for their own health more or less. This is seen in the 30 percent of patients who self-treat themselves. Another important aspect of the Ugandan experience was that while user fees were abolished in government health clinics, it was assessed only in Grade A clinics or hospitals. These are deemed necessary because Grade A clinics were supposed to provide efficient and better quality service (Government of Uganda, 2001: 27). The new policy was estimated to have generated a total of 4.41 billion shillings and the largest hospital, Mulago, generated Shs 1.4 billion. On that basis, it seemed true to argue that the degree of recovery through user fees was roughly 15 percent of the total cost. However, a careful analysis of the total revenue generated from user fees was not more than 3.6 percent of the total public health expenditure (Government of Uganda, 2001). Thus, consistently across Africa, the view that user fees are important sources of revenue for the government is highly debatable. Further, it has been argued that the "lack of clear understanding of how social insurance fits into the overall health care financing strategy[has] led to the neglect of preventative and primary care services" (Government of Uganda, 2001: 37).

Furthermore, as the evaluation team noted, it is difficult, if not impossible, to ask civil servants to contribute their earnings to a new social health insurance scheme. After all, they are taxed enough and are not satisfied with the services they receive. One major apprehension noted by those interviewed on the viability of such a program was their frustration with the current system. They were not convinced that the money will follow the patient. For example, several expressed dissatisfaction with their experiences with the retirement program (National Social Security Fund and National Insurance Company). Thus, while privatization and the use of other alternative financing strategies appear innovative, the experience from Uganda so far suggests that they are not working, or will not work. Increasingly, what appears to be useful in all this is a policy of decentralization and the use of local resources in planning and financing health care. The experience from Tanzania is illustrative and it is to this that we turn.

THE TANZANIAN EXPERIENCE

Tanzania has a long history of state intervention in health care. From its socialist objectives of the 1960s, culminating in the Arusha Declaration of 1967, the directive by the government has been that "health services should be made available to all Tanzanian at no cost to the people" (Ministry of Health, 1994: 18). This was followed by the nationalization of hospitals and a ban on private medical practice in 1977. This was perceived by the government as a way to guarantee equity and access to health with no regard to income or geography. However, as the Tanzanian economy declined, so did revenues and at the urgings of the World Bank, the government re-assessed its views on healthcare financing. User fees or cost sharing was introduced in July 1993. This was introduced as a way of supplementing governmental options in healthcare financing and also as a way to ensure efficiency in the delivery of health care. Cost sharing was introduced at the district hospital with mixed results. As already suggested, it has negatively impacted healthcare utilization. As with its use in health centers, it has been introduced with limited understanding of household perception on health-seeking behavior and households' willingness to pay (Hiza and Masanja, 1997: 5). One key aspect of this new policy was the decentralization of health services and their sources of funding. It was argued that for health services to be efficient, they must be run at the district level through the creation of the District Health Boards (DHB). Each district will develop its own health plan and objectives and institute other ways of generating resources and target its expenditure in the promotion and accessibility to health (Hiza and Masanja, 1997). Tanzania is currently experimenting with health insurance among civil servants. In 1999, the Tanzanian Parliament passed a bill to establish the National Health Insurance Scheme for civil servants. It was anticipated that it would be phased in gradually starting with a small percentage of the public sector workers. The specific provisions under this act were that the scheme will be mandatory and will cover employees, spouses and children or legal dependents not exceeding four family members and contributions will come from both the employer (3percent) and employee (3 percent) (Bituro, 1999). Preliminary assessment of the use of health insurance among teachers has concluded that while the idea is a sound one, its implementation has been thwarted. For example, it has been documented that some of the healthcare providers are unaware of this particular program and are not keenly aware of the existing payment models, leading some providers not to treat patients without payment up front. Some of the users of the plan have also complained about the services provided and some are frustrated with the abuses that they have received from healthcare providers, including long delays and inferior services (Quaye, 2004). As a result, an informant indicated that the system has not been popularized enough and it is most likely that the whole public insurance system will be done away with.

Increasingly, what appears to work for Tanzania is the primary healthcare approach, evidenced in the introduction of the Community Health Fund (CHF) as a way for communities to finance health services. The Tanzanian Health Sector Policy document states that the objective of the policy is "to improve the health and well being of all Tanzanians with a focus on those most at risk by ensuring that health services are responsive to the needs of the population" (Ministry of Health, 1994:1). As explicitly stated by Hemed (1999:219), "CHF is a rural health financing scheme in which households prepay a predetermined amount of money to cover health care services of house members." Experiences from other countries where CHF has been introduced suggest that community involvement in health care has been positive. Individual and community members report greater satisfaction with the services they received from these centers and generally believed that access to drugs has markedly improved. As reported by Hiza and Masanja (1997), the experience from Guinea Bissau suggests that the program has been quite successful in addressing the key elements of equity, cost and accessibility.

The specific forms included the provision of CHF cards for family members. This guaranteed their access to health services. In the CHF scheme, household members typically pay 5000 shillings ($5) per year. In Igunga district, the user fees for non- members is 1000 shillings ($1) (Hemed, 1999). In the CHF scheme, exemptions of poor households are given by village committees.

In their evaluation of the program in Igunga district where the scheme has been introduced, Hiza and Masanja (1997) reported that the scheme has made cheap prescription drugs widely available. The prepayment aspect of it made it worthwhile for families where employment was seasonal. Participants interviewed reported that the scheme was of great benefit to them. In terms of the limitations of the program, they stressed that communities were not adequately informed about the benefits of the program, leading to a reduced household participation of only 5 percent. Another concern raised was the fact that the scheme did not sufficiently address the problems of polygamous families. Since this family arrangement is a well-established practice, the scheme should have offered alternative arrangements for households as well. Another point mentioned was the limited range of health services available to the participants and the restrictive use of services to only health centers and dispensaries. Another concern voiced was the timing of the program. Since the premium cycle starts in June, it did not allow for greater participation by other members of the community because of the shot duration of coverage. From the perspective of the Ministry of Health, the initial evaluation of community health financing programs suggest that the program has been well received and that it has the potential of meeting the clear objectives of the Tanzanian government in protecting the most vulnerable groups in society. The cost- sharing aspect has been deemed appropriate and the fees assessed are not too prohibitive to affect access. Above all, patients have reported general satisfaction with the services provided, especially the availability of drugs. The involvement of the community in the design and implementation of the program has given the community a sense of ownership.

Given the fact that about 75 percent of Tanzanians live in the rural areas, CHF has worked very well in addressing the problem of access. The lesson from Tanzania is that the government can create an enabling environment through its decentralization programs and offer health resources to help communities meet the target of extending health services to the population.

This chapter has provided an overview of the role of cost sharing in health care in Africa. While cost sharing is theoretically sound as a health care financing strategy, it has not worked very well in the African context. As eloquently stated by Rice, "cost sharing is more burdensome on people with lower incomes... and its imposition leads to decreased service utilization, which in turn can impair health status" (Rice, 1997:418). What seems appropriate for Africans is the reinforcement of the primary healthcare programs, particularly the expansion of the community health financing models. The experience from Tanzania suggests that this is the route that Africa governments should undertake. This chapter also underscores the important role of national governments as enablers. Studies on the post-colonial state have charged that state with not being part of the solution, but very much a part of the problem. As others have suggested, the goal of the post-colonial state as sustaining the articulation of the economy to world capitalism and the creation of a 'bourgeois' class that serves the interests of capital is changing (Alavi, 1972). The very fact that a large percentage of the sources of funding directed towards primary healthcare come from external sources makes it difficult for African countries to exert strong influences on its distribution. As a practical matter, the post-colonial state in Africa should not only continue to establish lists of essential drugs, but they must double their efforts in seeking ways to strengthen the community financing initiatives. As observed by Canila, "Without the social protection of insurance schemes, the poor resort to out-of-pocket payment at the point when health services and medicines are needed" (Canila, 2003:3).

In a nutshell, very little is known about the various health care financing strategies in Africa. In an increasingly interdependent world, the cross-national experiences with alternative healthcare financing options offer a rich field for analysis. Unfortunately, with a few notable exceptions, such as Wang'ombe et al., (2002) evaluation of the use of social insurance health system in Kenya, most of the literature on healthcare financing has focused exclusively on user fees. There is, of course, a comparative healthcare financing agenda in Africa, but in general, it describes countries in isolation, or looks at the differences between systems, rather than at their interdependence. The understanding of health financing models must begin with the kind of nation-specific studies and comparisons undertaken in this chapter. The next chapter examines the theme of market reforms and the role of the state in health care financing and delivery.

Chapter Two

Market Reforms in Health Care and the Role of the State

In this chapter I outline factors that led to greater market forces in health care and decreasing role of the state in health care provisioning. This trend, it must be stressed, is not only unique to Africa. After all, rising health care expenditures in all Western countries over the last three decades have forced national governments to introduce market-oriented reforms in health care. For example in Great Britain, it was widely believed that an alternative system could be devised that retained the advantages of the National Health service while expanding consumer choice and reducing supply-side inefficiencies (OECD, 1995). This was achieved through the use of financial incentives such as diagnostic-related groups (DRGs) in health care. In a similar vein, the Dekker reform in the Netherlands and the Blum reform in Germany focused on the introduction of market- oriented systems in the delivery of health care. Thus, to address the problems of inefficient and lack of uncoordinated financing structures, the Dekker reform gave Dutch providers competitive incentives to produce cost-effective care and also streamlined the private insurance sector by creating a common risk-related insurance premium financed by the government (Quaye, 2007). Under the Blum reform, competition among German health care providers was encouraged through a diagnostic-related group based reimbursement payment system. Even in Sweden where health care is regarded as the responsibility of the public sector instituted a system of separate purchasers and providers and performance-based reimbursements (Quaye, 2007).

A clear shift in health care financing in Africa emerged out of the World Bank's World Development Report of 1993 titled, "Investing in Health." The report among other points, suggested that health improvement can be sustained through "the encouragement of market forces and competition in the health sector." Specifically, the report called for the following objectives:

1. Fostering an enabling environment for households to improve health;
2. Improving (as opposed to increasing) government spending in health;
3. Facilitating private sector involvement (Panos, Report, 1994:1).

Since the early 1980s, funding for the health sectors in most African countries has come from general tax revenues, donor support and private out-of-pocket household expenditures (Zikusooka, 2007). Indeed, the high cost of providing free care and the dwindling financial resources have forced governments to consider alternative financing strategies. This shift is made necessary because of the global burden of disease facing many countries. While developing countries account for 84 percent of the world's population, 18 percent of the world's income, and 93 percent of the worlds disease burden, they contribute only 11percent of the global health spending (Schieber and Maeda, 1997). Regrettably, the "single largest source of financing for health services is out-of -pocket payments, which exceed 25 percent of total health care expenditure in more than 75 percent of Sub- Saharan countries" (Mcintyre, et al., 2005). In response to these circumstances, African governments have introduced three methods of health care financing- user fees, community health funding and social health insurance.

The rather negative income effect generated by out-of-pocket payments has contributed to greater experiment in social health insurance. In the 2005 World Health Assembly resolution on "Sustainable health financing, universal coverage and social health insurance," it was made abundantly clear that social health insurance is the way of the future. Not coinciden-tally, in the early 1990s, several African countries introduced, at the very least some type of health care privatization. It must however be noted that private financing has long existed in Africa in the form of private-not-for-profit mission, faith-based organizations, private health practitioners, tra-ditional and complementary medicine practitioners in the informal sector (Schieber and Maeda, 1997). So what is the big deal about social health insurance?

As Zikussoka (2007:8) noted, "Social health insurance refers to compul-sory contributions into a health fund, made by mainly those who are formally employed, in return for a health care benefit package covering them and their dependents." Simply put, social health insurance is defined as "the reduction or elimination of the uncertain risk of loss for the individual or household by combining a larger number of similarly exposed individuals or household who are inclined in a common fund that makes good the loss caused to any one member" (Criel,1998:59). According to Shaw and Griffin (1995:54), "Health insurance is virtually the only practical instrument governments can use to get out of the expensive business of providing across- the-board subsidies for hospital care, thereby releasing funds for public health programs." Whether that is the case or not remains to be seen. Nevertheless, there are prudential reasons for using social health insurance as a health care financing strategy. After all, health insurance works to cushion the huge losses generally associated with a catastrophic illness or injury. Given the seasonal nature and the lack of regular incomes necessary to meet the huge financial bills associated with medical treatment, there is no doubt that insurance provides for families the peace of mind under extreme catastrophic illness. There are of course, different types of health insurance programs. Most insurance- based financing operate through contributions to social insurance earmarked for health care purposes. In the Netherlands, they are called 'sickness funds' and they are managed by private insurance companies with government control and regulation. In most cases, membership is compulsory only for people with a certain income level. Others take the form of a tax- based system such as the one in Great Britain. Under this model, the state assumes an increasing responsibility for financing through general tax revenues. Coverage of the population is more or less universal. The well known model is the private insurance which operates in a manner that corrodes the social solidarity principle of equity. Under this model, the nature of payment more often than not is based on the health status of individuals for it takes the form of risk- adjusted premiums reflecting the individual's health status. The benefit of risk-pooling is that it makes it possible for ordinary families to be able to afford the cost of health care. In situations where governments intervene to protect the most vulnerable groups such as patients with pre-existing medical conditions or the poor and the aged, private insurance offers one of the major ways of achieving equity and access in health care. As we have also learned from other countries, private insurance can encourage insurance companies to engage in patient skimming and dumping as well. On the other hand, one major drawback for using health insurance is the well known concept of moral hazard. Simply put, "moral hazard occurs when members of a health insurance plan use services more frequently than they would have had they not been members (Shaw and Griffin, 1995). This can be offset by asking consumers to pay part of the costs of their health care through co-payments for example. Health insurance has the potential to increase health care costs. In the USA, the fee- for –service payment system has contributed to the high cost of health care. On the demand side, since consumers access the health care at virtually no cost, they are more likely to demand more health services. On the supply side, physicians and health care providers are more likely to do more, given the fee –for service mode of payment. It creates in some sense, a perverse incentive for health care providers to do more.

Vogel (1990) in a comprehensive study of formal health insurance in Africa concluded that between 1971 and 1987, only seven countries had formal health insurance systems. Specifically, Vogel classified the prevailing health insurance arrangements as follow:

1. Those that provide universal free health care financed by national tax revenues.
2. Those that provide government-sponsored health care financed through a combination of general tax funds and cost recovery, as in Ghana.
3. Compulsory social security systems for the entire formal labor force.
4. Special health insurance funds for government employees, as in Sudan.
5. Those that provide a discount at health care facilities as well as those that mandate employer coverage of health care for employees.

Similarly in a World Bank survey of thirty-seven countries, fifteen countries had formal insurance systems in place (Shaw and Griffin, 1995). One important point stressed by Shaw and Griffin (1995) is the fact that private health insurance, no matter the structure or form, guarantees equity in health care. It also improve "economic efficiency, raise the quality of medical services, and allow consumers some choice in selecting and paying for their treatment "(Shaw and Griffin, 1995:77).

The Ugandan experience is illustrative. Between 2000/1 and 2005/6, per capita public expenditure on health, ranged from $6 to $10 (Zikuooka, 2007). As eloquently stated by Zikuooka (2007:9), "Although health services are provided free of charge in the public sector in Uganda, the quality of health services in the public sector is considered to be poor and large proportions of the population still access health services from the private sector where they pay out-of-pocket at the time and point of consumption." We will return to the specific details of the Ugandan design later. In my next discussion, I will review the literature on cost sharing or user fees in Africa.

Chapter Three

User Fees: A Special Issue for Health Care Delivery in Africa

In response to the World Bank recommendation that the principle of cost recovery be incorporated into the health care services in developing countries and consistent with the IMF and World Bank structural adjustment programs, user fees were introduced as part of the broader agenda for health care reform in Africa. The need for cost recovery in health care emerge out of the difficulty that African countries were facing in raising enough revenue to meet the free health care services they offer to their citizens. Another fundamental issue was the current state intervention in health care has been skewed in such a way that most government spending on health care has gone to the urban, mobile, highly educated elites at the expense of the rural and poor majority. After all, the bulk of government expenditure in health care subsidizes major government hospitals which are widely concentrated in the urban centers and cities serving most of the urban educated elites. The logical question is whether funds can be effectively mobilized to extend health services to the poor by asking the well to do to pay more for health services . Shaw and Griffin report that user fees in public health facilities help to promote equity because the demand for health care rises disproportionately with income. As Shaw and Griffin (1995:2) aptly noted, "it is important that government expenditures on health can be allocated far more cost-effectively, with the prospect of extending basic services to larger numbers of low-income Africans." According to Wang'ombe (1997:2) the major objectives for cost recovery are:

1. Increase total revenue for health through imposition of charges to users of public health services which were previously provided free of charges.
2. Improvement of coverage and quality of care available by the application of increased financial resource base for the health sector.

3. Enhancement of equity in the provision of healthcare by targeting certain expenditures on health care infrastructure for service packages for the poor and vulnerable population groups.
4. Improvement of service utilization patterns by controlling frivolous demand by directing services/choices for users through price and level of provision.
5. Increase efficiency in the provision of health care by making providers cost conscious and seeking to encourage cost effective techniques of provision of care.

Concerning user fees as a source of revenue generation, the evidence points to the fact that of the twenty–nine African countries that have instituted some form of cost recovery, about one-third see the mobilization of revenue as their primary objective (Shaw and Griffin, 1995). Tables 3.1 and 3.2 summarize the cost recovery structure in Public Health facilities.

As discussed in the previous chapter, further discussions on user fees have focused on the two important core values in health care- equity and protecting the most vulnerable groups of society. On the question of equity, research suggests that the effect of fees has been immediate and has negatively affected access to health care services. For example, recent evidence confirms that fees have acted as a barrier to service use by certain population groups (Wang'ombe, 1997). The Kenya study by Mwabu and Wang'ombe showed utilization drops of up to 38 percent. Similar trends have been observed in

Table 3.1.   How Much Do the Poor Gain from Government Health Service Expenditures in Africa? (percent)

	Primary Care Percentage of benefit of gained by:		Total Care Percentage of benefit of gained by:	
Country	Poorest population quintile	Richest Population quintile	Poorest population quintile	Richest Population quintile
Côte d'Ivorie (1995)	14	22	11	32
Ghana (1992)	10	31	12	33
Guinea (1994)	10	36	4	48
Kenya (rural, 1992)	22	14	14	24
Madagascar (1993)	10	29	12	30
Tanzania (1992-93)	18	21	17	29
South Africa (1994)	18	10	16	17
Unweighted average	15	23	12	30

Note: The percentages refer to the total financial benefits from government health care expenditures accruing to the poorest and richest population quintiles
Source: Castro-Leal, et al. (2000)

other African countries. One way out of this has been the use of exemptions to protect the most vulnerable groups but even this is fraught with problems. For example, fee exemptions have been found to be notoriously ineffective and has been beset with problems, including corruption. One important aspect of the cost recovery program which has gained much needed support has been the policy of retaining fees where they are collected. In this way, greater decentralization has allowed districts to decide how to manage the funds collected. This policy has been in operation in several African countries. In countries like Malawi, the revenue is split between the health facilities and the Ministry of health (Wang'ombe, 1999). Another important dimension to the user fees has been the recognition that the imposition of fees has led to better deliver of service and consumers have become more involved in their health care. They have demanded better services from their health care providers and providers have been more sensitive to the needs of their patients. This has been a welcome trend in the health care delivery system and a push back to the perennial "abuse" that patients experience at the hands of some of the health care providers.

In summary, user fees provide an important arsenal for most African health care systems. In countries where the program has been well designed and implemented, it has led to greater efficiency in health care and has also worked to achieve some measure of equity in health care. The major drawback for cost recovery programs has been its negative impact on health care utilization by those who are not able to pay. Perhaps, it is precisely for this reason that Uganda in 2001 abolished user fees in health services. As Shaw and Griffin rightly noted, "An important criterion for a successful cost-sharing strategy is whether increased revenues result in more regular supplies of essential drugs" (Shaw and Griffin,1995:52). It remains to be seen whether African governments have been successful at that. In all our discussions though the role of the state has not been well articulated. It is to this broader discussion that I turn to next.

The state is central to any discussion of health care financing strategy in Africa. Generally speaking the state has been defined as "a body that possess a monopoly over the means of force, as well as most of the means of sustaining the society through education and professional training" (Krause, 1996:22). Weber (1946b:78) defines the state as the organization whose essential characteristics is its monopoly of the legitimate use of physical force. The formation of states in Africa is premised (among other things) on the historical specificity of African societies, which arises from structural changes brought by the colonial experience, by alignment of classes, and by the superstructure of political and administrative institutions which were established in that context (Alav1. 1972). In his book, Thomas examined the nature of

Table 3.2.

S/N	District	Status	Problem	Recommendation	Remarks
9	Singida District Council	• CHF started in May 1998 • CHF contribution is 5,000/=per year per house hold. (HH) • Total household CHF registered January-June 2002 are 787. • Member of CHF registered from May 1998 to June 2002 was 7,521/= • Membership contributions to date Tshs. 13,607,000/= • Matching grant received Tshs. 10,208,500/= • Userfees collected Tshs. 9,957,000/= • NBC interest gained. Tshs. 177,537.60 • Total Tshs. 33,950,037.60 • Total expenditure Tshs. 15,343,200 • Balance Tshs.	• Most health facilities need to be rehabilitated. • Lack of adequate trained personnel. • Too much dependence on foreign aid. • Improper CHF records because of lack of trained accountant. • Unexpected resignation of DMO in 1999 and ill health and death of his successor in the year 2000/02	• Advocacy to leaders at different levels on advantages of CHF • Capacity Building to improve performance. • CHF to be taught in schools/colleges. • Extension of health facilities to village level. • Procurement of modern diagnostic equipment.	Fee level reasonable as per prepayment

		18,606,837.60 •There is a good collaboration with ELCT. There is a contract between the Board and ELCT health facilities to treat CHF members	
10	Iramba District Council	•CHF was introduced in 1997, implementation started on 1st June 1998 •CHF By-law in place •Membership has been fluctuating ranging from 2.4% - 5.3%	•Government health facilities are in poor state. •Membership contribution have been affected by dropouts, government employees who have joined NHIF

state and class formation in post-colonial societies. Drawing examples from Africa and the Caribbean, he stressed the importance of looking at the state as a historical materialist category based and shaped by both the process of internal development of class struggle and by the position that these societies and the classes within them hold in the global system of capitalism. Based upon this historical specificity, Thomas traced the changing role and conceptualization of the state from pre-colonial to post-colonial periods. Although, much of his discussion focused on the role of the state in post-colonial societies, he showed how the requirements of the colonial economy in cash crop production led to greater expansion of the state in the field of economic activity. Thomas argued that the authoritarian state emerged in response to the underdeveloped nature of the productive force. Given the absence of any developed elite class, the class that had access to political power under colonialism used the state machinery as a mechanism for consolidating its position and power (Quaye, 1996). Given the long history of military intervention in Africa, it can be argued that the military and the state bureaucracy cannot be viewed simply as instruments of a single ruling class, because the specific structural alignments which developed in the post-colonial situation rendered the relationship between the state and the social classes more complex. The essential problems for the state stem from the fact that it is established not by an ascendant, indigenous class, but by a foreign class. This is the point Saffu (1983:3) makes when he states that as "to the question, who dominates or rules the post-colonial states, the emerging consensus is that it is the for-

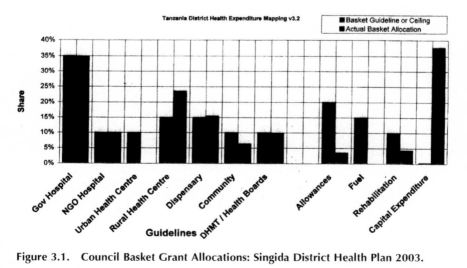

Figure 3.1.   Council Basket Grant Allocations: Singida District Health Plan 2003.

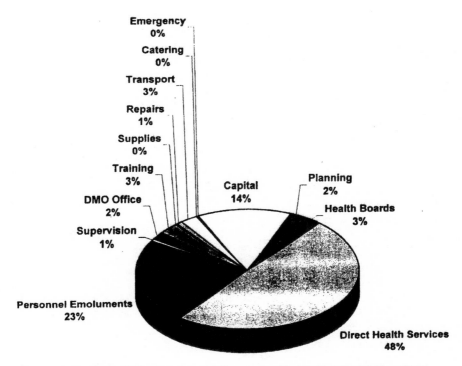

Figure 3.2. Total Health System Support Shares: Singida District Health Plan 2003.

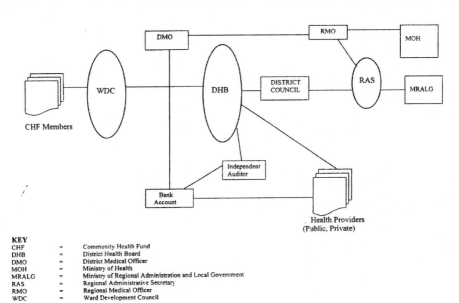

KEY
CHF   =   Community Health Fund
DHB   =   District Health Board
DMO   =   District Medical Officer
MOH   =   Ministry of Health
MRALG   =   Ministry of Regional Administration and Local Government
RAS   =   Regional Administrative Secretary
RMO   =   Regional Medical Officer
WDC   =   Ward Development Council

Figure 3.3.   Community Health Fund Operations Overview.

Table 3.3. Acheivements of National Systems of User Fees with respect of Three National Goals

Country	Increase Revenue	Enhance Efficiency	Improve Quality
Gambia	38% drug costs (90/91)	Same fee across levels	Drug availability improved, but still interruptions in supply
Ghana	5-6% recurrent costs (90/91)	Fee varies with level	Drug shortages continue following fee increase
Kenya	45% non-staff, non-drug operations budget at provincial general hospitals	Fee varies with level	User interviews suggest quality improvement
Lesotho	9% recurrent costs (91/92)	Fee varies with level and reduces for referrals	No clear pattern
Mozambique	? below target	Same fee across levels, waiver for referrals	No evidence
Zimbabwe	3.5% recurrent costs	Fee varies with level, no waiver	No evidence
Benen	43& recurrent costs in BI districts	No waivers	Drug availability improved at HCs
Burundi	?	Prepayment or fees	Drug availability improved at HCs
Cameroon	?	Prepayment or fees	Drug availability improved at HCs
Cote d'Ivore	7% MOH recurrent budget	Fee varies across levels	Drug availability improved at HCs
Guinea	Varies by region; up to 100% non-salary recurrent cost in some areas	Fees set locally	Surveys and focus groups suggest quality improvement at HCs
Mali	102% MOH recurrent budget	Fee varies across levels	?
Senegal	4% MOH recurrent budget	?	No evidence

eigners or owners of international capital who do." In response to the Berg Report engineered by the World Band and the IMF, several African countries swallowed the bitter pill of structural adjustment programs (SAPs). Among its specific objectives was the devaluation of local currencies, removal of sub-sidies, reduction in government expenditure and greater transparency in both government and the economy. It also for the first time led to the introduction of the user fees or cost recovery programs in health, education and other social service programs. In the area of health care, such directives eventually led to greater privatization in health care and a declining role of the state in health care. Whether this has worked or not, remains to be seen as we explore the experiences from three African countries- Uganda, Tanzania and Ghana.

Chapter Four

Health Care Financing in Uganda:
The Role of Social Health Insurance

The high cost of health care and the limited financial resources available for African governments have forced a re-ordering of health care financing in Africa. In most countries, per capita public expenditure on health care has declined. For example, in the period between 2000/1 and 2005/6, per capita public expenditure on health, ranged between $6 and $10. This number was below the estimated cost of (US $28) recommended by WHO (Zikusooka, 2007). At the same time, out-of -pocket expenditure on health constitute about half of all health care expenditures in Africa. Even in Uganda the 'demands from international donors for increased efficiency and competition are leading governments to play a smaller role in providing health care' (Panos Report, 1994, p.1). In the past decade, a confluence of forces has changed the nature of health care financing in unprecedented ways. The introduction of user fees has led to concerns about access and equity. One aspects of the financing structure that is less understood and used in Africa is social health insurance (SHI) - widely used in the Western world. Normally, SHI mobilizes funds for health care through contributions to a health insurance fund. The most common basis for contributions is payrolls, with contributions from both employer and employee. Traditionally in the United States, about eighty percent of the cost is covered by the employer and about twenty percent by the employee. In most parts of Europe and especially in the Netherlands and Germany, up to about fifty percent of the cost is paid by employees through a complicated cross-subsidization calculation. Generally, SHI is financed through compulsory premium payments on employed workers as a percentage of their wages. Thus, SHI is not automatically a universal program for all citizens. Those who are not in a position to make a contribution cannot hope to benefit from this program. What is typical in Canada and other parts of the

Western world is a general tax revenue system available to all, irrespective of financial situation (Rice, 1997).

In the whole of East Africa, with the notable exception of Kenya, very few studies have been done on the feasibility of using social insurance in health care delivery. Furthermore, studies conducted on the Kenyan use of social health insurance suggest that insurance programs by themselves do not adequately address barriers to access. In some cases, it might actually discourage the timely utilization of health services with severe implications for health. Both Uganda and Tanzania have had little experience with health insurance and currently no social health insurance scheme exist in Uganda. In 1999, the Tanzanian Parliament passed a bill to establish the National Health Insurance scheme for civil servants. It was anticipated that it would be phased in gradually starting with a small percentage of the public sector workers. Preliminary assessment of the use of health insurance among teachers has concluded that while the idea is a sound one, its implementation has been thwarted (Bituro, 1999). The Tanzanian experiment like that of other African countries, including Ghana, has not been properly evaluated. The Ugandan National Health Policy clearly places health financing reforms as elements supporting the objectives of reducing 'mortality, morbidity, and fertility and the disparities therein'(Government of Uganda,2001). To achieve this strategy, the policies call for the development and support of alternative financing schemes, such as health insurance.

LITERATURE REVIEW

In response to the structural adjustment programs engineered by the IMF and the World Bank (Huber, 1993), approximately 14 out of the 15 African countries surveyed by Gilson and Russell (1995) introduced user fees (or user charges), which are paid at the time of use to the provider who retains them partially or totally. These fees can be mere nominal amounts intended primarily to deter unnecessary service use by householders, or they can be more extensive, up to complete cost recovery. Thus, user fees have come to be seen as an important alternative to tax-based financing for government health services in Africa. This user fee financing structure has two models. The standard model has among its objectives the need to make health services more efficient and equitable. In this regard, the goal was to introduce sector changes and use other incentive methods to ensure efficient delivery of health services by health care providers. This has the intended goal of protecting the most vulnerable in society. For example, in its goal to achieve equity, the Kenyan government introduced a policy directive that exempted the poor

(Wang'ombe et al, 2002). The second model is the Bamako Initiative— widely used in Tanzania through a community financing program. The aim is to 'revitalize the public sector health care delivery system by strengthening district management teams and capturing some of the resources the people themselves are spending on health.' (Panos Report, 1994). This particular approach recognizes the importance of community involvement and health service decentralisation. As clearly documented (Mwabu et al.1998, Criel, 1998, Gilson and Russell 1995), user fees are highly regressive. It is more of a problem for the group supposed to benefit from the service since it has a negative income effect on the poor. As Criel (1998, p.40) noted: 'User fees create particular problems for farmers for whom income is highly seasonal.' In both Tanzania and Uganda, user fees have been associated with a decline in hospital and clinic use. In Kenya experience, user fees led to reduced attendance at government health facilities by 40 to 50 percent (Mwabu and Wang'ombe, 1998). Only private and mission sectors are currently charging in Uganda, which reduces the prima facie case for SHI to protect against financial risk and catastrophic costs.

Another objective for introducing user fees has been to reduce unnecessary health service use. Asking users to pay for a portion of the health service, no matter how nominal the fee, is intended to discourage excessive use of health services. As to the charge that user fees are a major source of revenue for hospitals, the evidence suggests that this has not materialized. Indeed, less than five percent of expenditure on health is derived from user fees. In short, the experience with user fees in Africa has been disappointing (Wang'ombe et al, 2002).

An alternative proposed in several African countries has been the implementation of a nationwide social health insurance scheme (the focus of this paper). While several African countries have explored the modalities of such a scheme, only Kenya has experience in implementing it. In 1967, Kenya passed its original legislation for the establishment of a government-operated health insurance scheme - the system of National Hospital Insurance Fund (NHIF), to cover hospital services. Under this system, NHIF operates as a traditional insurance, which serves as a third-party payer to certified institutions on a fee-for-service basis for inpatient drugs and medical services given to persons insured by NHIF. While NHIF has successfully pooled risks for a significant portion of middle and upper-middle income Kenyans, it has not been able to expand its coverage to include more Kenyans. The scheme also suffers from poor management and rampant corruption. It is estimated that less than 70% of expected revenue is being received by the NHIF. According to Wang'ombe et al (2002), this and other insurance schemes cover roughly 20% of the population. Furthermore, only three percent of Kenyan households use insurance to pay for medical care. Patients also reported that they were generally dissatisfied with the services provided under this scheme (Mwabu, 1998).

Recent Tanzania experience provides some insight into what is required to design a workable SHI in the East African setting. Tanzania began planning for SHI in the middle 1990s with assistance from the World Bank as part of the development of a new health system reform project. In 1999, the Tanzanian parliament passed a bill establishing National Health Insurance for civil servants. It was to be phased in gradually, starting with a small percentage of the public sector workers. The scheme was mandatory and designed cover employees, spouses and children as legal dependents (Bituro, 1999). Preliminary assessment of the use of health insurance among teachers has concluded that while the idea is a sound one, its implementation has been thwarted. For example, it has been documented that some health care providers are unaware of both this particular program and the existing payment models (Masanja and Hiza, 1997). Some users complained about the quality of services provided, and some were generally frustrated at the abuses in the system.

So far as we can tell, the only comprehensive study undertaken to assess the feasibility of the Ugandan SHI was undertaken by a team from the Harvard University School of Public Health and the Ugandan Institute of Public Health. In a report entitled, 'A Feasibility Analysis of Social Insurance in Uganda', the team concluded that: 'While social health insurance can improve health performance in Uganda, the conditions prevailing in Uganda as in many low-income countries may make the successful development of social health insurance (SHI) difficult and risky' (Government of Uganda, 2001, p.7). With that as a background, Ugandan perspectives of the introduction and their expectations of a social health insurance were explored. Consequently, this chapter explores the feasibility of developing social health insurance in Uganda and assesses the likely benefits and challenges in the introduction of SHI. The study addresses the following questions:

1. Is it possible for the Ugandan government to introduce an SHI that is satisfactory in terms of coverage, risk protection, and management of benefits, given the economic, social, and political conditions in the country and the constraints they impose? and if so
2. Are Ugandans ready for such a program?
3. Given the fact that a large number of Ugandans work in the informal sector and therefore less likely to contribute to a national health insurance scheme, what are the prospects for getting ordinary Ugandans to pay into a common scheme?

4. What should be done to those vulnerable groups who either cannot afford to pay or are unwilling to pay?
5. What do most Ugandans expect the program to cover?

METHOD AND DATA COLLECTION

To explore current views of Ugandans from all sectors of the population specifically, the term 'social health insurance' and what means for Ugandans were explored, notably:

• their views on the introduction of social health insurance in Uganda;
• what they expected insurance to provide by way of health services;
• who they felt should contribute to SHI financing and what specific contributions they are willing to make; and
• problems associated with the introduction of SHI and how such problems can be solved.

The data were obtained from a survey carried out in Kampala, Uganda in July 2005. Out of the hundred survey questionnaires, 74 were returned. To explore diverse perspectives, a strategy to elucidate the views of particular population groups was used. The questionnaires were distributed to volunteer participants at:

• Makerere University, Mulago Hospital;
• two less expensive hotels in the heart of Kampala;
• two up scale market (very expensive); and
• two low scale (less expensive) restaurants in Kampala.

Apart from the socio-demographic section of the questionnaire, they were open-ended questions. This allowed respondents to give detailed responses. Table 4.1 summarizes the respondents' social characteristics.

RESULTS

An overwhelming number of respondents understood the meaning and purpose of SHI. Over 98% respondents reported that social health insurance is a health service provided either by the government or by a private institution. As to what SHI meant to them personally, several of the respondents

Table 4.1.   Demographics (N= 74)

	N	%
Gender		
Male	36	49
Female	38	51
Age (years)		
25-35	42	56
36-45	12	16
36-46	8	11
56-65	3	4
65+	3	4

Table 4.2.   Religious Affiliation

	N	%
Protestant	22	30
Catholic	21	28
Muslim	11	15
Hindu	3	4
Other	14	19
No religion	3	4

Table 4.3.   Education

	N	%
High school	9	12
College	29	39
Vocational	6	8
Post Grad	15	20
Form Four	10	14
Elementary	1	1
No response	2	2

Table 4.4.   Residence

	N	%
Own home	27	36
Rent	28	37
Live with relative	13	17
Other arrangements	7	9

Table 4.5. Employment

	N	%
Employed	53	71
Unemployed	19	25
No response	2	2
Govt. employee	17	22
Self-employed	11	14
Family Business	1	1
Other (private)	24	32

mentioned that SHI is public insurance with the ability to support the poor and the needy. One respondent said that SHI means "safeguarding [myself and my family] from future health hazards like malaria or any other disease that might attack me." As for the benefit, several mentioned that SHI means the help one could get when sick, even any person from one's family: "it means, a [program] where people are given assistance for example, health treatment without one single coin given." For another "it was the provision of free medical treatment in all hospitals for citizens of Uganda." Another mentioned that it is "a system where an individual pays a small amount so that in case of sickness, the scheme can pay for one's treatment". One response also captures these notions "Social health insurance is a means of guaranteeing social health security." Some also see SHI as a scheme designed to provide free medical care to all citizens as well as allowing money to accumulate to help sick people as well as insuring one's life for bereavement purposes. A university student said: "social health insurance is a prepayment for health services." From these comments, it is clear that the majority of respondents have an appreciation of the role of SHI as a health care financing strategy. No differences in terms of attitudes between males and females or by age and or occupation were found. When respondents were asked what benefits social health insurance provided, a majority pointed out that the SHI should:

- provide free and timely health care;
- increase health care quality;
- improve health;
- offer free burial; and
- pay hospital bills, including prescription drugs.

Another stated that "after paying my contributions, I expect it to take care of my health risks." Several had a comprehensive view of SHI. For one it meant "providing all the medical care, emergencies, accidents for them and their families as well as helping my people with financial assistance and physical needs when I am dead."

We then explored the question of who should contribute financially to support the SHI's introduction. We had expected, given the increasing role of the state in health care services and the abolition of user fees in health services by the Ugandan government since 2001, to see the majority of Ugandans expecting the government alone to contribute to the scheme. We were surprised that only about half (58%) of the respondents believed that the national government should assume total responsibility for SHI financing. About 29% believed that employers should contribute financially to SHI for their employees. About 18% reported that they would be willing to contribute directly to SHI, which suggests that many Ugandans believe that employer contributions are essential. We asked our respondents whether SHI should be available to all Ugandans. An overwhelming number (80%) declared that the scheme should be made available to all Ugandan citizens irrespective of their ability to pay. Only 12% said it should not be offered to all. When asked to elaborate, one mentioned that "Ugandans has not reached that level yet and to provide SHI would mean that the government would have to fund it fully and this would strain the national budget." Others mentioned that rich people can take care of themselves so if it is provided by the government, it must be only for the less privileged. Only the poor and the old should benefit since not everyone can afford to pay insurance premiums. In response to the question on government fully funding the SHI program, several mentioned that Ugandans are poor and therefore cannot afford to contribute to the scheme. Some felt that SHI should be the responsibility of the government because health is one of the major components of an individual's wellbeing. Of those who felt that the government should pay, one said: "All Ugandans are prone to health-related problems and thus need the insurance." One mentioned that SHI is necessary because "It is very expensive to meet health costs and also because it secures people's lives."

On the level of contribution they are willing to make, 27% said they would be able to contribute between 1000 to 20,000 shillings monthly to the scheme. About nine percent reported that they would contribute between 21to 30,000 shillings a month and twenty-eight percent responded that they would contribute between 41,000 to100,000 shillings a year. We wanted to ascertain from our respondents what they felt were the likely problems and challenges if SHI was introduced in Uganda. One problem mentioned by the majority of the respondents was the need to sensitize Ugandans to the benefits of the program. Several reported that some people may become inattentive to their health and this can be overcome by sensitization: "you should deliver messages to the grassroots in order for people to know about the social health insurance." Some also mentioned the need to closely monitor the program so that it does not lead to mismanagement and corruption. Some made specific references to the level of corruption associated with the management of the National Social Security Fund (NSSF) as one way of how not to run the SHI scheme. For others, the political instability in northern Uganda must be addressed and solved as well as in Uganda. Generally, some were anxious to know when the scheme could be introduced. Another mentioned that "There is a problem of money because most Ugandans are low income earners and some Ugandans do not see the benefits of the SHI: "Many people do not understand why, if they do not fall sick during the year, their money is not returned to them. For a place like Makerere University, the scheme should be run by MUASA (Academic Staff Association). This will ensure transparency. Premiums should be deducted at source by the bursar." One recommend SHI's speedy introduction because there are so many people who cannot afford the current health delivery system. Additional funding to individuals with health risks would be a great relief to the government and the individual. In general, many reported their support for the introduction of social health insurance in Uganda, although some mentioned that coverage should be limited only to Ugandan citizens.

DISCUSSION

This study examined Ugandans' perspectives on the feasibility of the introduction of a Ugandan SHI scheme. While the study surveyed residents only from the nation's capital, Kampala, it nevertheless represents a general view of many Ugandans on the benefits of SHI. Our findings suggest that our sample of Ugandans are knowledgeable about the role and functions of a social health insurance. Many of our respondents reported that introducing a workable social health insurance will significantly improve access to health care and would provide other services and benefits that are currently not available to them. Most believed that the government should play an active role in the design and implementation of the scheme and that some employers should be forced to cover their employees by reforming the current value added tax system to allow companies to use tax income to finance the provision of SHI for their employees. What was unexpected was the large number of Ugandans willing and eager to personally contribute to such a scheme from their own funds. While several applaud the need and significance of such a scheme, they equally call for greater transparency in its design and implementation.

As a health financing strategy, very little is known about SHI schemes in Africa. But in an increasingly interdependent world, the cross-national experiences with alternative health care financing options offer a rich field for analysis. Unfortunately, with a few notable exceptions, such as Wang'ombe et al's (2002) evaluation of the use of social health insurance in Kenya, most of the literature on health care financing has focused exclusively on user fees and community health financing. There is, of course, a comparative health financing literature, but in general, it describes countries in isolation or looks at the difference between systems rather than at their interdependencies. Indeed, the understanding of health financing models must begin with the kind of nation-specific studies and comparisons that this article attempts to address. A central research question is: would social health insurance in Uganda, given the constraints on the national government be acceptable? Our research findings suggest that the Ugandan government should introduce a workable SHI in the coming years. As we better understand its role, the Ugandan experience provides a window on how to design a workable SHI scheme.

Chapter Five

Balancing Public and Private Health Care in Tanzania

While cost sharing has been used extensively in Africa, the nature of its use and the type of health care financing strategies has differed across the continent. While some African countries have depended on the community health financing scheme such as those in Tanzania and Kenya, relatively little is known about the history of social health insurance as a health care financing strategy in Africa. According to Wang'ombe et al (2002), insurance schemes cover about 20% of the Kenyan population. Both Uganda and Tanzania have relatively short history of using social health insurance as a health care financing option. So far as we can tell, Uganda does not currently have social health insurance in place. Tanzania have had four years experience with health insurance. In 1999, the Tanzanian Parliament passed a bill establishing the National Health Insurance Scheme for civil servants. It was anticipated that the scheme would be mandatory and would cover a small percentage of the public sector workers. It has been four years since the introduction of the social health insurance. In this paper, I surveyed a cross section of Tanzanians attending a professional meeting last year to reflect on this new financing strategy.

Specifically, in this chapter, I explore the perspectives of Tanzanians on the newly introduced social health insurance. I am particularly interested in assessing the benefits and challenges of this scheme on both the users and non-users of the scheme. The study addresses the following questions:

1. Will the Tanzanian population support the expansion of this scheme to cover all Tanzanians? And if so;
2. How much are Tanzanians willing to pay to finance such an expansion?
3. What should be done to those vulnerable groups who either cannot afford to pay or are unwilling to pay?

4. What role should employers play in financing health care?
5. What do most Tanzanians expect the scheme to cover?

METHOD AND DATA COLLECTION

To explore current views of Tanzanians, the term "social health insurance" and what it means for Tanzanians were explored, notably:

• What they expected social insurance to provide by way of health services;
• Who they felt should contribute to SHI financing and what specific contributions they are willing to make;
• Their understanding of what social health insurance meant to them; and
• Problems they associate with the current health insurance scheme and how such problems can be solved.

The data was obtained from a survey carried out in Dar es Salaam in February 2006 to participants attending the February Tanzanian Public Health Association Conference and to a meeting of a cross section of Tanzanians attending a benefit meeting in a local hotel. Out of the hundred surveys distributed, 57 were returned. Apart from the socio-demographic section of the questionnaire, they were open-ended questions. This allowed respondents to give detailed responses. Table 5.1 summarizes the respondents' social characteristics.

RESULTS

In this paper we wanted to ascertain the extent to which Tanzanians were familiar with the social health insurance system as currently configured in Tanzania. To access that, we asked our respondents to define what they understood the concept to mean. Over 85 percent of our respondents demonstrated through their responses that they have a good understanding and purpose of social health insurance. Several define social health insurance as a system that insures access to health care to beneficiaries enrolled in the plan. One respondent argues that SHI is "an insurance whereby communities are able to access health services through a prepaid cost sharing either through their own contribution or someone else and therefore do not have to pay right there while being treated at the hospital," Another states that SHI is "a system [which] ensures that those who are on government payroll are given health services because they contribute monthly through their salaries." For

Table 5.1.   Demographics (N=57)

Gender	N	%
Male	26	45
Female	27	47.3
No response	4	7
Age		
18-24 years	1	1.7
25-35	9	15
36-45	18	31.5
46-55	14	24.5
56-65	8	14
66+	6	10.5
Income		
21,000- 30,000	11	3.5%
61,000+	46	87%
Religious Affiliation		
Protestant	18	31.5%
Catholic	29	50.8%
Muslim	6	10.5%
Hindu	0	0
Other	2	3.5%
Own Home		
Own Home	36	63%
Rent	21	36.8%
Education		
'O' Level	8	14%
'A' Level	4	7%
College	28	49%
Vocational	0	0%
Post Graduate	16	28%
Should SHI cover all Tanzanians?		
Yes	42	82%
No	7	17.5%

another, "it means pooling risk of paying for health services by charging a nominal fee to many for the good of those who will be unlucky to get sick." Another respondent sees it as an "alternative source of health sector financing to alleviate overwhelmingly government expenditure on healthcare of its employees." It was also noted that SHI allows people who are members to access health services. It has the concept of cost sharing and it covers members' family members." Perhaps, one sums it well by stating that SHI is a "way of saving money for late use when in need of health services. It is like banking for health."

When respondents were asked to discuss what benefits social health insurance should cover, a majority pointed out that the SHI should:

- Provide free medical treatment for those who contribute or are members of the scheme
- Provide maternal services and to expand coverage for more than four individuals in the family
- Treatments, investigations and technological interventions and the provision of equitable health services at an affordable cost.
- It should take care of one's retirement needs as well since this is the time that health problems are more common
- Quality health care given timely near home or workplace or recreation site depending on where I will be and when I will need health care
- Cover all health service needs, including outpatient and inpatient care
- To render or enable me and my family access treatment whenever the need arises.

Another respondent in an answer to the benefits of SHI states that, "it should cover medical care, including consultation, lab investigation, prescription drugs, health education and advice. It should also provide "assistance in medical emergencies, e.g. Ambulance services, deliveries, major and minor operations and must include the whole family." For another, SHI should cover all [his] health care needs not covered under the National Health Insurance Fund. For example, dental care, eye glasses of ocular lens provision, x-rays and CT-scans. These should be offered to my family and my parents."

We explored the question of who should contribute financially to support SHI. We had expected, given the increasing role of the state in health care services, to see the majority of Tanzanians expecting the government alone to contribute to the scheme. To our surprise, 82 % of the sample reported that they would be willing to contribute directly to SHI. As a matter of fact, 19% of the sample reported that they would contribute 5000 shillings a month, 12% reported they would contribute 10,000 shillings. 8.5 % were willing to contribute 50,000 shillings a month and less than 25% mentioned that they will contribute 10 percent of their salary to SHI. About 17 percent reported that they will not be able to contribute. Among the non-contributors, about half mentioned that they were financially unable to do so because either they have retired, or they do not make enough money to contribute. We then asked whether the SHI scheme should be available to all Tanzanians. About 74% of the respondents believed that it should cover all Tanzanians. Only 12% said it should not.

On the question, what problems are likely to be associated with SHI in Tanzania, more than half of the respondents pointed to the low participation in the program. One respondent stated that, "most people are reluctant in contributing to the fund due to the lack of knowledge on what the scheme is for." Another mentioned that the health centers involved in providing these services do it partially because not all diseases are treated under this situation. Some also mentioned the resistance from the community members. In addition, some reported that "some members may not fall sick therefore there is a problem if no premium guidelines are introduced to refund portion of the money." Another respondent referred to the current National Hospital Insurance Fund (NHIF) bottle neck in assessing the relevant service provider as one way of not how to use SHI. About one third of the sampled population mentioned that drugs are not available in many hospitals and there are no pharmacy shops for the NHIF to buy drugs for patients as stipulated in the guidelines, particularly in the rural areas. Some mentioned corruption and favoritism among insurance agents as barriers to effective utilization of the SHI. Another respondent mentioned that, "There should be a baseline mechanism to determine who can/ cannot contribute and waivers should be introduced." Others reported the lack of involvement at the local community levels. As one respondent argued, "the success of the program depends on involving the communities from the beginning so that they can understand their roles and responsibility to SHI sustainability." Another mentioned that "money was deducted from [him] about two years [from his salary] without service. Others complained that the system does not cover medicines and does not cover all family members. Above all, some mentioned poor communication, inadequate funds, poor strategic plan and poor knowledge of SHI by most Tanzanians as key barriers to full utilization of the scheme.

Similarly, they mentioned misuse of services, mediocre quality of service, overpricing by providers and under-staffed health facilities are issues arresting the use of SHI in Tanzania. Some stressed that poverty is rampant in Tanzania and therefore majority of Tanzanians will not be able to contribute effectively. As one indicated, "not everyone can contribute, so few people could be left out unless the government agrees on 100% subsidy. If this is addressed the question is what criteria can be used for determining the subsidy?" Another point raised by one of the respondents was that there should be a flat rate to ensure that the rich are not overburdened.

Next, we asked our respondents to assess what the likely outcomes would be if employers were required to provide health insurance for their employee, a policy that is widely utilized in the western world. About half of the sample was pessimistic about employer contributions. Several mentioned that it is not in the best interest of employers to do so since employers are after profit and employees are very concerned about their basic pay. Others stated that conflict of interest may preclude this from working as employers may deduct the cost from employees' salary. Some indicated that employers through contract with insurance company may skim patients, only willing to insure only healthy patients at the expense of others. They also mentioned that employers are less likely to pay for very expensive treatment or laboratory texts. The rate of contribution set by the Act is 6% of employee's salary shared equally by employers and employees. In a response to this question, another mentioned that not all employers will be in a position to contribute for their employees. Even for those who may, they may limit the medical coverage.

Finally, we asked our respondents to reflect on the viability of the SHI program in Tanzania. While in principle, majority of the respondents were in favor of extending the program to cover all Tanzanians, several cautioned the system should be well planned and effectively managed if it is to make any headway in the rural areas. About half mentioned that employers and employees should be asked to contribute a certain percentage of their incomes to finance the scheme. Several mentioned that Tanzanians should be well informed/empowered on the program for its sustainability. Others mentioned the computerization of health services, shortening documentation, and easy access to health care providers as challenges to be addressed. From the perspective of another respondent," SHI should be introduced after a participatory approach at the community level. There should be a feasibility study conducted to ascertain the willingness and ability of participants to pay for the service. The health insurance system must be publicly funded, be self sustaining, and must cover all segments of the Tanzanian population. As one put it, "it [SHI] should encompass all economic groups and it should not be tough on the poor who need it the most." They also mentioned the need to sensitize the public and employers to the benefits of the SHI scheme and that it should cover non-civil servants too.

DISCUSSION

This study examined the perspectives of Tanzanians on the use of social health insurance as a health care financing strategy in Tanzania. While the study surveyed participants attending a national conference in Dar es Salaam, it nevertheless represents a general view of many Tanzanians since the sample participants came from different parts of the country. Our findings suggest that many saw SHI scheme as significantly useful in addressing barriers to health care access in Tanzania. Most believed that the government should play an active role in expanding coverage to other segments of the population by funding the scheme. They also pointed the need for the government to ensure that all Tanzanians, irrespective of their financial circumstances are covered. They suggested that a flat rate should be paid by those able and capable while creating a safety net for those who cannot. In all this, the health services should be better planned, services effectively delivered, and greater sensitization of the Tanzanian population must be undertaken to ensure a successful implementation of the scheme for all Tanzanians.

CONCLUSION

Health insurance has been used extensively in Western societies and it constitutes the major part of health care financing. This is not the case in Africa. While Kenya provides a good example of the role of health insurance in health care, the available literature suggests that health insurance schemes pose several problems for governments. One such drawback is its limited coverage. In Kenya, about 3% of Kenyan households actually use health insurance to pay for medical care (Wang'ombe et al., 2002).The Kenyan experience does suggest that insurance programs by themselves do not adequately address the barrier to access. In some cases, it might actually discourage the timely utilization of health services with severe implications for health. Our study suggests that while the fundamental structure and support for the expansion of the Tanzanian health insurance plan is in place, much needs to be done to assess the impact of the current SHI on health care equity and access. While the community health service schemes appear to have worked well in the rural communities, it is not quite clear whether the SHI introduced to cover civil servants has worked the way that they should. It is impossible to accurately answer this question given the rather small sample size of this paper. Perhaps, a larger study, comparing the perspectives of current participants will yield useful information for assessing whether Tanzania is ready for further expansion of the SHI program. As we better understand the role of SHI as a health care financing strategy in Africa, the Tanzanian experience provides a window on how to expand a SHI scheme. In the next chapter, I explore the nature of health care financing in Ghana with a discussion on the introduction of the National Health Insurance Scheme.

Chapter Six

Health Care Financing in Ghana: Role of the National Health Insurance Scheme

Private financing represents almost half of all health care expenditures in developing countries (Schieber & Maeda, 1997). In most cases, these expenses are incurred through out-of-pocket expenses, user fees, community health funding and most recently in Africa, private health insurance. While health insurance has been used extensively in Western societies and it constitutes the major share of healthcare financing, this is not the case in Africa (Quaye, 2004).

Kenya provides a good example of the role of health insurance in health care. The available literature suggests that health insurance schemes pose several problems for governments (Quaye, 2004). One major drawback is its limited coverage. For example, the only-well established insurance is the National Hospital Insurance Fund (NHIF). This insurance covers only those in the public sector. According to Wang'ombe et al, (2002), the current insurance and other insurance schemes cover roughly 20% of the population.

The Kenyan experience does suggest that insurance programs by themselves do not adequately address the barrier to access. In some case, as demonstrated by the Kenyan study, it might actually discourage the timely utilization of health services with severe implications for health. Another drawback in terms of the use of health insurance is that it is by its very nature regressive. In other African countries, governments prefer a flat rate contribution such as the 3% contribution by employees and employers in the Tanzanian case than that based on need and income earnings. This suggests that a large number of Africans who utilize the health services do so with their own money (Quaye, 2004).

Historically, in response to the structural adjustment programs engineered by the IMF and the World Bank, several African countries introduced user fees (or user charges), which are paid at the time of use to the provider who retains them partially or totally. In Ghana, it took the form of what became known as "cash and carry" system. As clearly documented (Mwabu et al., 1998; Criel,1998;Gilson and Russell, 1995), user fees are highly regressive and it is more of a problem for the group supposed to benefit from the service since it has a negative income effect on families (Quaye,2007).

Another objective for introducing user fees has been to reduce unnecessary health service use. Asking users to pay for a portion of the health service, no matter how nominal the fee, is intended to discourage excessive health services' use. The charges that user fees are a major source of hospital revenues are not borne by the evidence (Wang'ombe et al., 2002).

In the past five years, several African countries have experimented with a nationwide social health insurance (SHI) scheme (the focus of this paper. For example, in early 2003, the Ghanaian parliament passed the National Health Insurance Act (NHI) outlining plans for a healthcare system that would guarantee universal coverage to all Ghanaians, irrespective of ability to pay (Singleton, 2006).The scheme went into effect in March 2005. The scheme allows for the creation of district mutual health insurance schemes, private commercial health insurance schemes and private mutual health insurance schemes and stipulates the provision of health services by these schemes as determined by the National Health Insurance Council (Singleton, 2006). The schemes receive subsidies from the National Health Insurance fund (NHIS 2003: III.33.2), financed through a 2.5% tax on all commercial expenditures and transactions, 2.5% of every person's contribution to the Social Security and National Insurance Trust Fund (SSNIT), money allocated to the fund by Parliament and other funds obtained from investments, grants, donations and other voluntary contributions. Under the scheme, those working in the formal sector make an automatic contribution to the scheme (as part of the 2.5 % deducted from the SSNIT fund contribution), while those in the informal sector pay a graduated amount depending on their assessed income level (Singleton, 2006).

In a policy speech by President Kufour, he asserted that," a robust health delivery program was integral to Human Resource Development and the achievement of the UN's Millennium Development Goals." (Kufour, 2008). He also announced that 48 % of the population, representing 9 million individuals are full members of the scheme. It is also projected that by the year 2013, all Ghanaians will be covered. While I applaud the government for this laudable goal, there has been relatively little research done to ascertain the perspectives of users and non-users of this scheme in Ghana.

To assess the role of such schemes in Ghana and to assess the perceptions of users and non- users, a large scale survey was undertaken in the summer of 2007.

The study addresses the following questions:

1. Is the current NHI scheme meeting the health needs of Ghanaians in terms of coverage, risk protection and benefit management?
2. How well informed is the general population on the benefits and drawbacks of such a scheme?
3. Are Ghanaians, those not currently enrolled, eager and willing to join?
4. Given that a large number of Ghanaians work in the informal sector and therefore less likely to contribute to a national health insurance scheme, what are the prospects for getting ordinary Ghanaians to pay into a common scheme?
5. What should be done for those vulnerable groups who either cannot afford to pay or are unwilling to pay?
6. What role can be played by health care providers and what do most Ghanaians expect the scheme to cover?

DATA COLLECTION

To assess the views of Ghanaians, a survey was conducted in Accra and in the surrounding towns in the summer of 2007. Five hundred questionnaires were randomly distributed to Ghanaians residing in the following areas; Adenta, East and West Legon, Airport residential area, Kokomlemle, Adabraka, Odorkor, North Kaneshie and Madina. The sample was carefully selected to represent the diversity of both the ethnic and class divisions in Ghana. The sample was a true representative of the Ghanaian population. The questions explored the following themes:

* Their views on the introduction of Ghana's NHI;
* Who they felt should contribute to NHI financing and what specific contributions they are willing to make;
* They were also asked the evaluate the services provided under the scheme and to ascertain whether the scheme was a better alternative to the previous "cash and carry "system; and
* Problems associated with the current scheme and how such problems can be solved.

Apart from the questionnaire's socio-demographic section, the rest of the questions were open-ended. This allowed respondents to give detailed responses. Tables 6.1-6.9 summarize the respondents' social characteristics.

Table 6.1.

	N	%
Gender		
Male	255	51.0
Female	245	49.0

Table 6.2.

	N	%
Age		
18-24	146	29.2
25-35	162	32.4
36-45	107	21.4
46-55	47	9.4
56-65	25	5.0
66+	13	2.6

Table 6.3.   Religious Affiliation

	N	%
Faith		
Protestant	349	69.8
Muslim	35	7.0
Catholic	87	17.4
Other	29	5.8

Table 6.4.   Suburb

	N	%
Achimota	32	6.4
Adenta	55	11.0
Chorkor	38	7.6
Labadi	30	6.0
Jamestown	31	6.2
Other (Legon, Madina, Airport)	314	62.8

Table 6.5.   Education

	N	%
Elementary/Primary	46	9.2
Junior Secondary School	105	21.0
O' Level	21	4.2
Senior Secondary School	103	20.6
A' Level	22	4.4
College	131	26.2
Vocational School	34	6.8
Post-Graduate	17	3.4
Other	21	4.2

Table 6.6.   Income (Cedis)

	N	%
0-500,000	114	30.7
501,000-1,500,000	112	30.2
1,501,000-2,000,000	52	14
2,001,000-2,5000,000	35	9.4
2,501,000-3,000,000	12	3.2
3,001,000-3,500,000	12	3.2
3,501,000-4,000,000	4	1.1
4,001,000-4,500,000	4	1.1
4,501,000-4,999,999	7	1.9
5,000,000+	19	5.1

Table 6.7.   Are you employed?

	N	%
Yes	360	72.0
No	140	28.0

Table 6.8.   Who is your employer?

	N	%
Government	107	21.4
Self-Employed	164	32.8
Family Business	26	5.2
Other	84	16.8
No Response	119	23.8

Table 6.9.   Are you enrolled in National Health Insurance Plan?

	N	%
Yes	166	33.3
No	332	66.7

Note: (N=500)

RESULTS

The results show that 51% of the respondents were male and 49 % were female. More than half of the respondents (61.6%) were in the age group of 18 to 35 years. Overwhelmingly (69.8%), identified themselves as Protestants, with 17.4 % identifying themselves as Catholics. About two thirds of the sample came from areas other than the immediate vicinity of Accra, the nation's capital. Most striking, about 66.7% of the sampled population do not subscribe to the insurance scheme. About one third (33.3%) are subscriber of the National Health Insurance plan. Approximately, 75% of the sampled population earn between 500,000 cedis to two million cedis. More than half of the respondents have a minimum of high school education with only 21% percent working as government employees. About two-thirds of the population either are self-employed or they own their own businesses.

We wanted to ascertain the extent to which Ghanaians were familiar with the National Health Insurance scheme as currently configured in Ghana. To examine this, we asked our respondents to define what they understood the concept to mean.

Over 98 percent of respondents showed in their answers that they have a better understanding and appreciation for the meaning and purpose of the NHI scheme. Majority of respondents (98%) define NHI as contributions mobilized to serve as a guarantee on health care and enrollees expects the government to contribute to the financing of NHI. A 36 year old male from North Legon stated that the "NHI scheme is a means by which the government subsidizes medical bills for citizens in the country." Another stated that the NHI scheme is "a way of mobilizing funds for unforeseen sickness." For another, it is financing the nation's health through contributions by everyone." A 45 year old female from Legon defines NHI as the, "the prepayment of hospital bills partly by the individual and the employer and government to promote good and quality health care." For another, NHI is "money set aside with the government to insure health circumstances and expects family members to contribute to the scheme." Another respondent states that NHI is "banking your health through contributions into a common fund." For another, it is a "system to replace cash and carry and hence provide free medical care based on your subscription at a reduced price." Most saw the NHI as an initiative by the government to help all citizens to settle health bills at a minimum rate through government subsidization. From the perspective of another respondent, the NHI "provides free medical care after enrolling under the scheme." Majority of respondents see the scheme "as an initiative by the government to insure one's health in order to attain health care even when one does not have money for that service or care."

When respondents were asked to discuss what benefits NHI should cover, over 99 % pointed out that the NHI should:

• Provide good health care for all kinds of sickness.
• Provide prompt and fast delivery on health care and expects the scheme to provide drugs for all types of sicknesses and help subsidize medications which are very expensive.

- Provide periodic check-ups in the hospitals for beneficiaries.
- Expects NHI to allocate part of the scheme's fund to help combat the breeding of mosquitoes in the country and inter alia, help prevent malaria.
- Expects NHI to provide quality medicine, irrespective of the cost and must allow contributors to attend any hospital and not the ones only within their own localities. Expects that NHI will provide more government hospitals in most communities to reduce the distance people travel to get to the health care center or hospital.
- Expects NHI to provide emergency health or urgent treatment on accidents and expects the scheme to cater for the unemployed people free of charge.
- Expects employer to contribute to health care and expect NHI to pay for medical bills and all surgical operations.
- Provide maximum health care services, free consultations, better treatment, free medication, utmost attention to patients and counseling services.
- Expects the NHI card to be accepted nationwide through a computerized system.
- Expects the health workers to treat me well whenever I attend the designated hospitals with my NHIS card.

Of the 332 (66.7%) of the respondents not currently enrolled, all of them expressed their willingness to contribute to the scheme. The average contribution current non-users were willing to contribute ranged from 500,000 to 1.5 million cedis a year. This is illustrative of the samples ability and willingness to pay.

We next asked our respondents (users and non-users) to comment on problems with the scheme as currently configured.

For the current users of the plan, majority of them (89%) reported the delay in receiving identity cards for the scheme. They also decry the fact that the card is limited to specific health cases and it is not portable to other districts.

Another concern voiced by the majority of respondents was the poor quality of service received by NHI members. Several mentioned that "sometimes patients are not likely to get medicines prescribed by doctors and they are therefore forced to buy the medicines themselves. Another user stated that, "health care providers discriminate against users of the scheme and prefer those who pay cash on the spot. For another, it is important for doctors and nurses to improve their interpersonal skills when dealing with patients. As bluntly pointed out by one respondent, "the rude attitudes of medical workers, especially the nurses to patients with NHI cards must stop." They also discuss the fact that health care providers unduly delay offering services to the NHI members as they prefer to attend to people who are paying cash. As one puts it, "all patients should be treated equally rather than side lining those with NHI policies in the hospitals." Further more, it was pointed out that those with the insurance cards are not well catered for in certain hospitals and to overcome this, there must be supervisors at each hospital to make sure these people are well catered for." For another, "the way patients with insurance cards are treated in hospitals if it is not corrected, it may stop people from joining the scheme." For another, "current managers of the scheme for the past two years should be jailed for poor management of the scheme." Another stated that the reluctance of health care providers to attend promptly to card holders may be due to the fact that the government will sometimes delay in releasing funds to the hospitals.

Another concern was raised about over invoicing by health care providers. As one respondent pointed out, "The scheme must come out with a definite billing for services rendered since some hospitals are charging high bills which does not square with the services rendered." Another mentioned that "health personnel who extort money from patients for their personal gains must be checked and penalized and some hospitals still collect money from patients (that is from those approved by) NHI scheme."

Finally, we asked our respondents to reflect on the viability and the challenges facing the scheme in Ghana. While in principle, majority of the respondents expressed their willingness to join and were generally in favor of extending the scheme to cover all Ghanaians, several cautioned that the system as currently configured should be better tailored and effectively managed to meet the health needs of the population. When non –users were asked why they have not yet joined the scheme, more than half reported that the procedure to become a member is cumbersome and a lot of them do not know the real benefit of the scheme. They also mentioned those who contribute now are denied expensive drugs and are made to wait for a long time to collect the medicine. paracetamol). Among the other obstacles mentioned included the following

- The services provided under the scheme are not comprehensive and the premiums are prohibitive for most Ghanaians.
- Need to make the scheme compulsory, rather than voluntary. This will ensure that citizens get the same kind of care.
- Need to expand the pool of health care providers to both government and private health care providers, including faith –based clinics.
- NHI agents who register people should carry ID cards for identification purposes
- At health centers, the person in charge of the NHI is not around and we are therefore forced to pay cash or wait for them.

- There should be a nationwide computerized system so that one can use one's card everywhere.
- Greater degree of transparency in the whole operation of the scheme so that people do not feel that their contributions are being spent irresponsibly.
- Corruption in the supply of drugs or medication should be checked.
- Government should provide additional funds to ensure the purchase of more effective and expensive drugs.
- There is discrimination against members of the scheme; they take proper care of those with cash instead.
- Some of the registration centers are charging more than they are supposed to charge registrants.
- The mentality of not taken care of government properties should be done away with as it will ruin the scheme.
- Portion of the money paid by contributors should be refunded if they do not fall sick or do not attend any health center in the year, or the money should be applied to the following year's premiums.
- Irregularities in the amount one is asked to pay; it varies from place to place but the same services are rendered at health centers.
- The NHI is a good initiative introduced by the government since it is really meeting the health needs of the public as compared with the "cash and carry" system.

DISCUSSION

This paper has examined the perspectives of Ghanaians on the introduction of the National Health Insurance scheme as a health care financing strategy. While the study participants were drawn from the nation's capital, it nevertheless represents a cross section of the entire population since every conceivable group can be found in Accra. Although we did not specifically ask for the ethnic identity of respondents, the selection of these suburbs were designed to reach the diversity of the general population. The findings confirm that many saw NHI scheme as a significant innovation in the provision of health care by the government. Majority of the respondents enthusiastically support the scheme and are willing to contribute to the scheme provided they can be guaranteed better quality of service. They prefer this system over the prevailing cash and carry system. Several decried the attitudes of health care providers and believe that greater sensitization should be conducted to ensure that health care providers are fully integrated in the delivery of health services. The evidence suggests that one of the major barriers facing the successful implementation of the scheme is the competing parallel system where health care providers are more eager and willing to treat those who pay for their health services at the point of delivery. Several Ghanaians mention their reluctance to enroll simply because the scheme is not portable and it is not compulsory. About half of the respondents also mention the long delay in the processing of their cards and decry the shortage of drugs at prescribed health centers and pharmacies. Perhaps one of the major obstacles facing the scheme is the lack of a nationwide computerized system to allow health centers easy access to member's records. There is no doubt that greater transparency is necessary for confidence building among beneficiaries and health care providers. Several of the respondents worry about the politicization of the scheme believing that the scheme will be terminated by an incoming government. There is also the danger of over utilization of health services since virtually members receive care free at the point of access. While this is a problem typically of all health insurance plans, one is not sure if co-payments should be introduced as well. The danger for introducing such a plan would be that it may render the scheme ineffective. There are however prudential reasons for ensuring that users of the scheme have better access to quality service and that health care providers do not favor those who pay user fees at the point of access. The major challenge facing the Ghanaian government is how to make the scheme financially viable. It has been suggested that the scheme be made compulsory, nationwide and that it should solicit the private/non governmental clinics in providing these services.

CONCLUSION

Relatively little research has been done to assess the role of health insurance as another alternative to the community based health financing systems in Africa. While health insurance has been used extensively in Western societies and it constitutes the major part of health care financing, this has not been the case in Africa. For the past five years, several African countries have introduced social health insurance as another form of health care financing strategy. Ghana, like Tanzania has been experimenting with this new form of financing and other countries such as Uganda is exploring the feasibility of introducing one. The paucity of research on this in Africa is a grave concern. While national health insurance schemes do not eliminate all the barriers to access, it provides for low income countries one effective way of insuring the population of the country through individual and government contributions. After all, given the disease burden in Africa and the limited resources of African governments, a broader vision of expanding health coverage through the private sector is long overdue. African governments must be encouraged to seek ways of meeting the goal of universal access to health care. As we better understand the role of health insurance in Africa, the Ghanaian experience provides a window on how to expand health coverage to millions of Ghanaians.

Chapter Seven

The Role of Community Health Funding in Health Care Access in Africa: Lessons from Tanzania

Community health funding grew out of the Bamako Initiative in 1987 where African Health Ministers adopted the resolution that the primary goal of meeting the health care needs of the population was through the "financing of health services through community participation in revolving drug fund" (Hanson and McPake, 1993:267). Specifically the Health Ministers agreed to:

- Encourage social mobilization initiatives to promote community participation in policies on essential drugs and maternal and child health at district level;
- Ensure a regular supply of essential drugs of good quality and at lowest cost, to support the implementation of the primary health care;
- Define and implement a primary health care self funding mechanism at district level, especially by setting up a revolving fund for essential drugs (Hanson and McPake, 1993: 267). For Tanzania, the interest in community health funding coincided with the government's overall national health policy of seeking alternative means of expanding health care coverage in the face of falling tax revenues, increased budget deficits and debts. While cost sharing has been introduced in 1993 at the level of referral hospitals and at regional and district hospitals, relatively nothing has been done at the community level to fund health care. As a result of this confluence of forces, in 1996 in Igunga district, the first pilot project on the area of community health funding (CHF) was introduced in Tanzania. On a general level, CHF is designed as a mechanism for providing additional funds for financing health services in rural areas of Tanzania (United Republic of Tanzania, 1999).

DEFINITION OF COMMUNITY HEALTH FUND (CHF)

It is a district-based, voluntary prepayment scheme, designed to complement other financing mechanisms with a goal of improving access to health services and to empower communities to participate in taking care of their own health (Ministry of Health, 2001).The fund enables households to receive health care for one year without any extra cost. This objective as outlined earlier on is consistent with the overall Bamako Initiative. It is seen as a strategy for long term financial sustainability and intended to raise revenues and ensure effective resource use through the development of community management capacity, and thus permit self-reliance (Baraldes & Carreras, 2003). The features of the CHF include flat rate membership contributions, pro-poor exemption policy, flexibility in choice of providers, efficiency and cost containment advantages and its compatibility with local autonomy and fiscal decentralization goals (Ministry of Health, 2001). Specifically, the fund expects:

- Household contributions which range from Tsh 5000/ to 15.000/ depending on council's decisions or agreement and on the basis of people's affordability and willingness to pay.
- Households unwilling to prepay, contribute in a form of user fees when seeking medical services. For this reason, user fees are set according to level of a health facility.
- Those who are unable to contribute are identified by the community, exempted, and given membership cards similar to those who have prepaid.
- Government matches the household's contributions.
- Membership is voluntary.
- The CHF reimburses health care providers for the health services rendered.
- Flexibility in choice of providers to the CHF members, but in reality members have been restricted to receive services in facilities in their wards.
- There is a district, village health board that oversees the program.
- Membership is open at any time. This encourages families to join when they realize the benefit of the scheme.
- CHF has successfully followed the partnership approach in solving health problems of the community as it involves the public sector, NGOs and the communities.

The CHF is enshrined in Tanzanian law, through the CHF Act of 2001. Currently, 69 out of 98 districts have established CHFs and improved access for members without the need for out-of-pocket payments at the time of requiring services.

In an interview conducted among Coordinators of Community Health Funding in five districts Arusha, Kigoma, Igunga, Mwanga and Singida) , it became clear to me that the fundamental principle governing the establishment of the CHFs were adhered to. In all districts, they all recorded increased growth in the number of membership of the scheme. In Iringa, the CHF was started in 1999 and operated from the Kimmolo District. It covered employees of the district council. Funds were raised through contributions by employees and from matching funds from the government. Non – members were required to pay 1000 shillings ($1) per episode. The CHF members pay 5000 shillings ($5) and it covers all family and children under 18 years. What is striking aspect about all these plans were the enlistment of faith-based organizations (FBO) and local dispensaries in the provision of health care services for the members. The CHF also provided prescription drugs for local schools. A review of the financial statement for this district revealed that the CHF is making significant improvements in the quality and access of health care and it is within budget. By June last year, the plan showed that the district had 6 million shillings in the bank. They were able to use the surplus money to expand out-patient departments and also used some of the money to pay for the services of a watchman (for security purposes). Part of the surplus was used for building repairs and maintenance of maternity wards and for prescription purchase. Regarding challenges facing the CHF in Iringa, it was mentioned that the introduction of CHF changed the way in which health services were delivered. For example, before the introduction of this scheme, the local district has its own CHF board but it was changed in 2004. They also indicated the tendency among some of the health care providers to overcharge the district councils for the health services provided. They also complained that some of the services were not covered under the CHF. For example, diagnostic services were not covered. Currently, there are about 56692 members covered under the CHF scheme. In Kigoma district in western Tanzania, three districts have established CHF schemes with 24, 600 members actively enrolled. The services covered by the scheme included: prescription drug purchase, medical supplies, provision of clinical and lab technicians and for physical improvements. The source of funding came from the basket fund (members' contributions), matching funds from the government and donor/NGOs support. They reported increased enrollment because of better services provided by health care providers and the degree of sensitization and involvement of the local communities in the planning and implementation of the scheme. In Sindiga District that the author visited in 2007, there were about 30,000 members. Members were generally satisfied with the services provided. In a study by Garimo (2007) evaluating the high drop out of community health fund members in Igunga district, he reported that among the factors contributing to the high drop out from the scheme were shortage of prescription drugs in government health facilities and limited financial means because of the seasonal nature of employment. For example, in some communities, especially in the tobacco and cotton growing areas, cooperative unions that buy their products do not pay them on time and in some cases they have to wait for months to be paid. This delay makes it difficult for them to have the needed cash to pay for the premiums. Another problem identified by Garimo (2007) was the fact that health care providers access fees at the port of service and are less likely to take and treat CHF members, given the prospective payment system structure of the CHF system.

From my readings of the CHF in several districts in Tanzania it has become abundantly clear that Tanzania has worked very hard to provide a workable system in the midst of current financial problems. The design implemented in several districts took into account the economic status in the areas. For example, the household contributions ranged from 5000 shillings ($5) in Iunga, Nzega, Kilosa, Sindiga Rural and Iramba to 7000 shillings in Sonega. In Hanang, household members paid 10,000 shillings. In Mbinga, they are assessed 15,000 shillings per household (Ministry of Health, 2001). It was also reported that non members paid the equivalent of between 1000- 2000 shillings per hospital visit. Another provision was the pro-poor exemption policy. Under this policy, membership cards were issued to those unable to pay. The community through the village heads are charged with the responsibility of assessing the poor in their respective communities and to approve these exemptions for the poor. In meeting the overall goal of protecting vulnerable groups in Tanzanian society, all under fives, pregnant women and the poor elderly have free access to public health facilities. There are however, several problems that must be addressed to ensure wider coverage under the scheme. One major barrier to toe rather low participation rate is the fact that membership to the CHF as currently configured is voluntary. The community member has a choice to either pre-pay or pay user fee to access health care services. While this ensures that household members can have easy access to health care, the voluntary nature of the system does not allow the fund to spread its risks and thereby reduces the benefits of such an insurance scheme. Other challenges faced by CHF include:

• Weather conditions and poor harvest contribute to low membership enrollment.
• Low prices for agricultural products lower the income of the community.

- Community awareness. Advocacy and sensitization is a concern.
- Qualified staff. Health facilities lack qualified and technical staff. This leads to patient/ client dissatisfaction due to poor quality of health services.

In expanding coverage of the CHF, it is argued that other options should be explored, particularly in pegging the contributions on the basis of the actual rather than projected earnings of members, given the conditions of poor harvest and unpredictable harvest season. In addition, the following are important steps to be taken by the government;

- Community awareness of the scheme. There should be greater sensitization and awareness of the benefits of the CHF.
- Availability of quality health services. One concern mentioned for the rather low participation is the poor quality of the government health facilities that they are required to use. In my conversation with community coordinators, they mentioned that patients would rather not enroll and take their chances when sick by accessing health services at the private or faith-based clinics since they are of superior quality.
- Transparency in managing funds. While this has not been a major barrier, some coordinators called for greater accountability and transparency in the use of membership funds.
- Exemption of the poor and the most vulnerable groups. This is currently been done but there is no uniform structure in place at the various district councils.
- Voluntary or compulsory to increase membership? In general, health insurance schemes work best when they are compulsory required but in developing countries such as Tanzania where the bulk of the participants are more likely to work seasonal and in the informal sector, forcing them to enroll will be difficult and may lead to low utilization of health care services.

In conclusion, the fundamental principle underlying the community health fund is a sound one. In 2007, 69 of the 98 district councils have established the CHF. This has improved access to health care services. The scheme has allowed the Tanzanian government to address its fundamental commitment of extending health care coverage to rural communities in Tanzania. In a comprehensive study undertaken by the Ministry of Health and Social Welfare in 2007 on the theme of "Community Health Fund: Best Practices Workshop Report" identified these key points.

- The review found varying enrollment patterns between different councils. While membership grew on some districts, it declined in others primarily

because of low household incomes, perceived poor quality of public facilities, the broad exemption policy; and the negative attitude of health care
workers towards patients.

- Regarding protecting the poor, it was argued that the exemptions created
  a perverse disincentive for households to join the scheme. The need for
  greater membership in order for CHF to effectively play its risk- sharing
  and cross subsidization role, and to avoid adverse selection, was mentioned.
- Regarding the management and accountability of the scheme, the review
  raised concerns about the limited awareness of performance of specific
  schemes, and the risk of having no CHF members in the Council Health
  Service Board and the ward Health Committees. They also identified short-
  ages in prescription drugs and the limited extension of the scheme to areas
  served by faith-based organizations or private for-profit facilities.

In summary, there are three potential problems with the expansion of the
CHF as it is currently configured. It is voluntary and not sensitive to income
earnings of members. Another problem is the perceived view that the services
provided under the scheme are of low quality and that the scheme is not comprehensive enough in providing all the required and needed services. There
appears to be less transparency in how revenues are collected and distributed.
There is the need for a viable system that will ensure that those in the informal
can be encouraged to join the fund.

Chapter Eight

Health Care Financing Strategies: Lessons from Abroad

According to Wang'ombe et al., (2004:1) "measures that improve health policies in Africa can substantially increase human development in the continent and contribute to poverty reduction." Sub Saharan Africa is confronted with several challenges- poor economic record, extreme poverty, scourge of AIDS, low life expectancy and high infant mortality rates among others. Yet for the past five decades, African countries have been bitterly disappointed with the performance of their health delivery systems. Policies designed to promote greater access to health has not been successful. In the past two decades, several African countries in their attempt to achieve the broad millennium of poverty eradication and infant and mortality targets, have encouraged the development of the private health sector as a way to further meet this goals. In the midst of these reforms, the linkage between the public and private health sector has not been well integrated. While several African countries have experimented with both private and public provisioning in health care, in general, it describes countries in isolation, or looks at the differences between systems rather than at their interdependence. The understanding of health financing models must begin with the kind of nation specific studies and comparisons presented in this book. In a thought provoking article by Thomas Rice titled, "Can markets give us the health system we want?" he stated that, "the belief that we should start with the principles of fairness, and then proceed to considerations of efficiency, is also the foundation upon which most other health care systems have been built" (Rice,1997:399). Among other points, he argued that "payments towards health care should be related to ability to pay rather than to use of medical facilities... and that access to and receipt of health care should depend on need, rather than on ability to pay" (Rice, 1997:399). In Africa, health care financing has taken three approaches. First, there is the widely used cost recovery system. While

61

some African countries have used user fees as an additional source of raising revenue, the literature is depleted with examples about how it has not worked. Rather what is widely known is that user fees by its very nature are regressive on the poor and has negatively affected access to health care. Furthermore, insurance and user fees have proved ineffective in expanding health services to the majority of those in the informal sector (Wang'ombe et al., 2004). The poor quality of health facilities in public health centers has also discouraged citizens from joining.

Regarding social health insurance, it is clear that it is limited in its coverage because primarily it is designed for those who work in the government sector. Most African countries have a short history in the introduction of social health insurance. In the countries studied in this book, they only have had just 6 years experience with the scheme.

Perhaps what is well known and appears to have a wider impact is the community health fund. As described in the last chapter, Tanzania seems to have done a good job in implementing the CHF. While the overall impact has been positive, there are still rooms for improvement. In other countries such as Thailand, a number of different financing strategies have been introduced. For example, the Universal coverage scheme introduced in 2001 and tax based covers those not currently employed by the government. Other schemes have included a purchaser-provider split, introduction of capitation payments for outpatient services and greater use of a diagnostic related groups, and reinsurance for accident and emergency costs (Ministry of Health and Social Welfare, 2007). Under the Universal coverage scheme about 80% of rural residents have been covered under this scheme. The scheme focus on health prevention and health promotion but faces difficulty in its financial sustainability.

Another country where the private–public partnership has worked is in Rwanda. Under the Rwanda Community Based Health Insurance program, 70 % of the population is covered. Contributions per person is estimated at $2, with a co-payment of 10% which is payable at each of the level of the health system, except for the poor who are fully subsidized by the government (Ministry of Health and Social Welfare, 2007). Similarly in Gujarat India, a scheme called SEWA covering 170,000 members, mostly poor women in the informal economy. This particular insurance covers not only health but also life and includes husbands and children. Two payment options are available. There is an annual premium of approximately $ 3 US dollars for each member and slightly less for a family member. Under this scheme both inpatient and outpatient health services are covered. Currently, the members pay out-of-pocket expenses and they are then reimbursed by SEWA upon submission of relevant documentations.

In the Phillipines, the PhilHealth, the national health insurance company covers about 74 of the population. To increase the pool of membership, micro-financing groups and other NGOs were encouraged to join. The scheme has worked very well in areas with better health facilities and thereby ensuring that members have better access to quality health care services. The question is if these countries have been able to expand health coverage through the existing public-private partnership, how come that some of these African countries have not been able to do so? As we have argued throughout this book, the introduction of social health insurance has been new in Africa and has been in operation for less than a decade. Tanzania and Ghana introduced social health insurance scheme as a health care financing strategy in the last six years. Uganda is yet to formally introduce one as yet even though they have conducted several feasibility studies about how and when to implement a workable system. Using user fees and health insurance schemes as alternative ways for delivering health care is here.. The challenge is for African countries to implement best practices in this area. Obviously, Tanzania and Ghana can learn from other successful countries in the developing world, including the welfare states in Europe. From my investigation of the private–public partnership in health care, it has become clear that African countries have a long way to go in incorporating health insurance schemes as viable alternative and in some cases, complementary to the already established user fee strategy they embraced in the early 1980s. The major barriers to effective acceptance of the social health insurance model has been the limited appreciation for the fundamental philosophy of social health insurance. In Kenya, even with the widespread use of private health insurance, a study conducted by Wang'ombe concluded that only 3 percent of households actually use insurance to pay for medical care. Part of it is the general view that the services provided through this scheme has not been well accepted because of its poor quality. These were observed in the three countries studied. Another major problem facing further utilization of the insurance schemes have been the delay in the issuing of identity cards and what is perceived to be rude attitudes of medical workers, especially the nurses and the delay in reimbursing health care providers for their services. Another issue that has to be addressed is the need to make the services comprehensive. In the end, greater sensitization to the benefits of the health insurance program will encourage greater participation by the people.

References

Alavi, H. "The State in Post Colonial Societies: Pakistan and Bangladesh." *New Left Review* 74 (1972):59-81.

Agyepong, I. "Reforming Health Service Delivery at District Level in Ghana: The Perspectives of a District Officer." *Health Policy and Planning* 14,1 (1999):59-69.

Bituro, S. "Development of the National Health Insurance Scheme for Civil Servants: Key Features of the Scheme." *Proceedings of the 18th Annual Scientific Conference of the Tanzania Public Health Association* Dodoma, 1999.

Canila, C. "Models of Health Care Financing. *Asia Pacific Consumer* 30 (2003):2-6.

Collins, D.H, Quick, J., Masau, S., Kraushaa, D.L., "Health Financing Reform in Kenya: The Rise and Fall of Cost Sharing." *Management Science for Health, Stubbs Monograph Series* No.1 (1996).

Cornia, A., Richard, J. Frances, S. *Adjustment With a Human Face* Oxford: Clarendon Press, 1990.

Criel, B. *District-Based Health Insurance in Sub- Saharan Africa.* Belgium: Studies in Health Services Organization and Policy, No.9, (1999):33-130.

Gilson, L. "The Lessons of User Fees Experience in Africa."*Health Policy and Planning* 12(1997):273-285.

Government of Uganda *A Feasibility Analysis of Social Health Insurance in Uganda* (Draft Review): Kampala, Uganda, 2001.

Gwatkin, D. "Free Government Health Services:Are They The Best Way to Reach the Poor?" Paper presented at the meeting of the World Bank, Washington. DC,(2003): 1-13.

Gwatkin, D. Poverty and Inequalities in Health within Developing Countries: Filling the Information Gap." *In Poverty and Inequality in Health: An International Perspective.* D'Leon and G.Walt, eds. London, Oxford University Press, 2001.

Gwatkin, D. "The Current State of Knowledge about Targeting Health Programs to reach the Poor" Washington, DC. : World Bank, February 2000 (http://www. worldbank.org/poverty/health/library/targeting.pdf)

Garimo. I. "Factors Contributing to High Drop Out of CHF in Igunga District" Paper presented at the Tanzania Public Health Association Conference, Dar Es Salaam, 2005.

Gilson, L., Russell,K, Buse,K. "The Political Economy of User Fees with Targeting: Developing Equitable Health Financing Policy." *Journal of International Development* 1995.

Huber, J. "Ensuring Access to Health Care With The Introduction of User Fees: A Kenyan Example." *Social Science and Medicine* 36 (4) (1993): 485-494.

Hanson, K and McPake, B. "The Bamako Initiative: Where is it Going." *Health Policy and Planning* 8 (3): 1993:267-274.

Kuffour, J. "Health Care Integral to Human Development." *Health News* (2008):1.2.

Leppo, K, "Strengthening Capacities for Policy Development Strategic Management in national Health Systems." Background paper Prepared for the Forum of Senior Policy Makers and Managers of health Systems. Geneva, World Health Organization, 2001. Equitable Health Financing Policy." *Journal of International Development* 7 (1995): 369-402.

Ministry of Health (2003) *National Health Insurance Act* Accra, 2003.

McIntyre, D. *Health Care Financing and Expenditure in South Africa: An Economic Evaluation* Ph.D Dissertation , Cape Town, University of Cape Town, 1997.

Ministry of Health. *Quantitative Evaluation of CHF Igunga Pretest (Including Singida Rural District* Kapinga and Kiwara (eds). Institute of Development Studies, Muhimbili University College of Health Sciences, 1999.

National Health Insurance Fund. *Actuarial and Statistical Bulletin of June 2004* Dar Es Salaam, Tanzania, January, 2006.

National Health Insurance Fund. *Actuarial and Statistical Bulletin of June 30th 2006* Dar Es Salaam, Tanzania, July 2007.

Mwabu. G. Mwanzia, J. & Liambila, W (1995) "User Charges in Government Health Facilities in Kenya: Effect on Attendance and Revenue." *Health Policy and Planning* 10: 164-170

Quaye, R. "Planning the Health Care System in a Decade of Economic Decline." *Crime, Law and Social Change* 16 (1991): 303-311.

Quaye, R. "Paying for Health Services in East Africa: A Research Note." *Social Theory and Health* 2 (2004): 94-105.

Quaye, R. "Health Care Financing in Uganda: The Role of Social Health Insurance." *International Journal of Health Care Quality Assurance* 20, No. 3 (2007):232-239.

Republic of Uganda. *National Health Accounts For Uganda: Tracking Expenditure in the Health Sector* Kampala, Uganda, Ministry of Health, 2000.

Republic of Uganda. *Assessment of Public Expenditures for The Health Sector in Uganda* Kampala, Uganda, HealthNet Consult, 2005/06.

Rice, T. "Can Markets Give Us the Health System We Want?" *Journal of Health, Politics, Policy and Law* 22, 2 (1997):383-508.

Schieber, G. & Akiko Maeda *A Curmudgeon's Guide to Financing Health Care in Developing Countries* Conference sponsored by the World Bank, Washington, DC. 1997.

Singleton, J. *Negotiating Change: An Analysis of the Origins of Ghana's National Insurance Act.* Sociology Department, Macalester College, 2006. (*http://digitalcommons.macalester.edu/soci_honors/4*

Shaw, P and Griffin, C. *Financing Health Care in Sub-Saharan Africa Through User Fees and Insurance.* Washington, DC. The World Bank, 1995.

United Republic of Tanzania. *Community Health Fund in Tanzania: Experiences From Igunga Pretest District and 9 CHF Roll Over Districts.* Ministry of Health, Dar Es Salaam, July 2001.

United Republic of Tanzania. *Community Health Fund: Operations Guidelines* Ministry of Health, Dar Es Salaam, Tanzania, 1999.

United Republic of Tanzania. *Community Health Fund: District Health Plan Model.* Ministry of Health, Dar Es Salaam, Tanzania, 1999.

United Republic of Tanzania.*Community Health Fund: Design* Ministry of Health, Dar Es Salaam,Tanzania 1999.

United Republic of Tanzania. *Community Health Fund: Best Practices Workshop Report* Ministry of Health and Social Welfare. Dar es Salaam, 2007.

United Republic of Tanzania. *Community Health Fund: Best Practices Summary* Ministry of health and Social Welfare, Dar Es Salaam, 2007.

Wang'ombe, J., Germano. M., Benjamin, N, Octavian. G (2002). "Financing Medical Care Through Insurance: Policy Lessons from Household and Community Level Analysis in Kenya." *African Development Bank* 14 (2002) : 75-97.

Wang'ombe, J. "Cost Recovery Strategies: The Sub Saharan Africa Experience." Paper presented at the International Conference sponsored by the World Bank, Washington, DC, 1997

Wang'ombe,J., Okello,D.,Mwabu,G., Munishi, G. *Improving Health Policy in Africa* Nairobi, University of Nairobi Press, 2004.

Zikusooka, C. *Assessment of Willingness to Pay for Social Health Insurance in Uganda* Kampala, Uganda, HealthNet Consult, 2007.

Index